MW00446549

DEVELOPING EFFECTIVE PASS PROTECTION SCHEMES

Stan Zweifel

Brad Boll

© 2001 Coaches Choice. All rights reserved.

Printed in the United States.

No part of this book may be reproduced, stored in a retrieval system, or transmitted, in any form by any means, electronic, mechanical, photocopying, recording, or otherwise, without the prior permission of Coaches Choice.

ISBN: 1-58518-319-9

Library of Congress Catalog Card Number: 00-106284

Page layout and cover design: Paul Lewis
Cover photo: David Gonzales

Coaches Choice
P.O. Box 1828
Monterey, CA 93942
www.coacheschoiceweb.com

To all the players I have coached the past twenty-five years, without you it would not have been possible.

To all the coaches I have worked alongside, starting with my college coach at the University of Wisconsin-River Falls, Mike Farley, and continuing through all of the others, thanks for all that I have learned.

__Stan Zweifel

To my parents who have always supported me whether I deserved it or not.

To my brother, who is also my best friend.

To Valerie, my soon-to-be wife, who already has an idea of what it means to be a coach's wife.

To the three men who have taught me most of what I know about the game of football, Stan Zweifel, Mike Curtis, and Pat Martin.

__Brad Boll

ACKNOWLEDGEMENTS

Thanks to Dr. Jim Peterson and Coaches Choice for helping me put my passion into words.

___Stan Zweifel

Thanks to Stan for giving me the chance to do something that I never thought possible.

___Brad Boll

CHAPTER 1

WHAT WE BELIEVE
ABOUT PASS PROTECTION

Undoubtedly, the long touchdown pass tops the list of football's most exciting offensive plays. A long scoring pass can change the complexion of a football game in a moment, restore the confidence of the most frustrated offensive unit, and demoralize even the most dominant defensive front.

Fans love the play for its simplicity. They admire the purity of Bret Favre dropping back into the pocket and showcasing his arm by launching yet another bomb deep down the far sideline into enemy territory. They appreciate the artistry of Jerry Rice hauling in a short pass and running clear, down the middle of the field, between the hash marks, well behind the coverage of the defensive secondary.

Given the opportunity, head coaches and offensive coordinators can seemingly design a pass pattern to defeat any defensive secondary coverage. In the attempt to gain an advantage, offensive units can line up in any of several different formations, trade a tight end across their formation, shift the running backs out of the backfield prior to the snap of the ball, use motion to get a favorable personnel match-up, or simply overload a zone. Regardless of the strategy employed, every pass pattern ever developed has included a route to be run by the primary receiver which appeared to be a sure completion when first drawn on the blackboard or put to paper.

Unfortunately, come Friday night or Saturday afternoon, most high school football coaching staffs become satisfied when a mere fifty percent of these well designed pass patterns actually result in a completion. The authors of this book firmly believe that most of the unproductive passing plays in any football game do NOT fail to produce results because the patterns themselves break down or the individual pass routes are not well thought out. On the contrary, the vast majority of these ineffective pass plays fail to work because the quarterback simply does not have enough time to make an accurate read, or because his protection does not allow him enough time to deliver the football when and where it needs to be thrown.

Successful offensive minded football coaches do NOT approach the passing game by concerning themselves only with formations and patterns. They realize that a talented quarterback and gifted wide receivers do not necessarily guarantee an effective passing attack. They know from experience that they must give significant consideration to their offensive linemen, and to the soundness of the pass protection schemes that will be used in conjunction with the particular pass plays that they want to run.

When considering a pass play for the first time, competent and responsible offensive football coaches should be far more concerned with how the offensive linemen are going to effectively protect the quarterback during the play than with the depth that the flanker needs to be when he reaches the break point in his route. The first question asked of any coach suggesting a pass play of any type should be, "How are we going to protect it?" If any part of the answer to that question includes the words, "we do not play against defenses that do that," or, "we handle that by throwing it hot," then there should be a significant amount of valid skepticism regarding the potential effectiveness of the play in the minds of reasonable offensive football coaches.

The authors of this book have several strong beliefs about offensive football in general, and throwing the football in particular, including the following:

We are not going to allow our quarterback to get hit in the face. If the quarterback begins to lose confidence in himself or in his protection, then he can no longer be an accurate passer or an effective leader of the offensive unit. Nothing diminishes the confidence of a quarterback more than getting hit. Our entire offensive unit understands that the primary goal, whenever we attempt to throw the football, is to keep the pass rush away from our quarterback. The players assigned to the protection scheme know that they are expected to do whatever it takes to carry out their responsibility in order to protect our quarterback.

We are going to account for every potential defensive pass rusher and not allow any player to get a free path to our quarterback. Our protection schemes will be sound. If we cannot account for everything that a defensive opponent may do, then we will NOT run a particular pass play and risk a defender coming unblocked and hitting our quarterback. Obviously, our quarterback will get hit when there is a physical mismatch up front and one of our offensive linemen gets beat by a better defensive player. Nevertheless, we will NEVER run a play unless our protection scheme can account for every potential pass rusher within the structure of the opponent's defense. Against some defensive opponents, our fourth and fifth receivers may never get released because they have to be kept in to block as part of the protection scheme.

There are worse things than an incomplete pass. Next to getting hit, the worst thing for a quarterback's confidence is throwing an interception. When we call a pass play, we do NOT expect to complete a pass 100% of the time, but we DO expect to remain in possession of the football 100% of the time. We expect our quarterback to correctly identify the secondary coverage on each play, and we NEVER want him to force the football into coverage. If no receivers are open, the pass rush is closing in, AND the quarterback has time, then we expect him to throw the football safely away and save our field position. If he is hurried or rushed, then we want the quarterback to secure the football with both hands and take a sack rather than throwing the football out of rhythm (risking an interception), or getting hit while trying to escape and turning the football over to our opponent.

Throwing it hot is never a good answer. Releasing five receivers into the pass pattern and throwing it hot on every down does NOT lead to consistent offensive production. However, if the defense decides to align eight or nine players inside the tackle box and three receivers are involved in the pattern, then we are forced to account for the eighth pass rusher with our eighth player—the quarterback. In these situations, we will, out of necessity, build a hot read into the pattern. We will specify exactly who the defender is that we cannot account for, and, if he comes, throw the football to a receiver running a predetermined blitz protection hot route. We do NOT do this by choice, but the popularity of today's attacks, bear, blitz, charge, pressure, up, and stunt fronts, gives us little choice. When we are forced to use a hot read, we teach the quarterback to locate the defender that we cannot account for is aligned within the structure of the defense.

You have to be able to run the football. While a few teams will win some games solely because of their ability to throw the football in a key situation, winning teams will be successful because of their ability to run the football and play sound, aggressive defense. Good football teams traditionally do two things very well: they run the football on offense, and they stop the run on defense. No passing offense ever developed can completely overcome shortcomings in these other areas. Additionally, the style of offensive attack that is used to move the football on the ground will have a tremendous impact upon which pass protection schemes are most easily integrated into the offensive package.

The execution of the offensive linemen and the soundness of the pass protection scheme are the most important parts of any pass play. A strong armed quarterback and great receivers with sprinters' speed will NOT be effective weapons against a physical defensive front that consistently gets pressure on the quarterback. Hurries, tipped passes, batted balls, and colliding with the quarterback as he releases the football will disrupt an offensive unit as much as sacking the quarterback. The structure of the wide receiver routes in any pass pattern are irrelevant because any competent coach can design a play to take advantage of a given defensive secondary coverage. The most important part of any offensive pass play is NOT the pattern of routes run by the receivers, but the pass protection scheme used by the offensive linemen to protect the quarterback. Implementation of sound protection schemes can make any offensive unit more efficient.

Any team can get better at throwing the football. There has been a tendency among successful high school football programs in our state to line up with two tight ends in two-back or three-back formations. They hang their hats on successfully running the football right at opponents, pounding the ball right at the heart of defenses. When these teams meet in the playoffs, the outcome of the games is often determined by who is most effective at throwing the football. As a result, even wishbone teams that only throw the football twice a game can benefit from the implementation and execution of sound pass protection schemes. By selecting a sound protection scheme and getting repetitions at implementing it versus a variety of defenses at practice, any offensive unit can become better at throwing the football.

The hardest thing for a high school offensive lineman to do is pass protect. So many high school offensive linemen play in systems that require them to be aggressive, physical, and get off the ball in order to effectively block the run game, that they are unable to maintain the proper balance, center of gravity, leverage position, and weight distribution when it comes time to pass protect. Because many of these linemen are asked to run block much more often than pass block, they never become comfortable with their pass protection techniques. Part of this problem results from the fact that the techniques that make an offensive lineman a great run blocker do not necessarily help him as a pass protector.

The use of multiple formations, motions, shifts, trades, and other surprises can force defenses out of the fronts, blitzes, stunts and/or coverages from which they get the greatest pressure on the quarterback. Each opponent that an offense faces has definite tendencies regarding what types of things they like to do in order to get pressure on the quarterback. They will each have favorite defensive looks that they like to give on third down. They will each prefer certain coverages in throwing situations. Once an opponent has been scouted and that information is known, it is a relatively simple matter to design plays and formations that will force them to get away from what they like to do in order to remain sound against particular offensive adjustments.

The effective use of screens and play action pass schemes can counter the speed of an opponent's best pass rusher. Not only are these types of plays effective, but they do not require the implementation of a protection scheme of any kind because they can be run while simulating one or more of an offense's base running plays.

This book has been written from an offensive perspective that draws upon, and reinforces these beliefs. It is really the adherence to these beliefs that led to the development, implementation, and use of the schemes discussed in this book. We think that the schemes described in this book have been successful because of the fact that they emphasize our beliefs, which we believe are crucial to the success of any effective offensive football attack.

The purpose of this book is to offer coaches at all levels of football basic, effective, and sound pass protection schemes that are easy to teach to their players. We believe that these pass protection schemes can be incorporated into any offensive system or individual pass play to improve the overall efficiency of any offensive unit.

This book is NOT meant to serve as an offensive playbook. While we will occasionally use various pass patterns as examples in diagrams when we discuss particular pass protection schemes, they have simply been chosen at random. We have made no effort to breakdown any individual defensive secondary coverage. Every offensive football coach has a relatively short list of his favorite pass plays against the coverages that they traditionally see from week to week. We intend to provide coaches with an effective means to run these bread and butter plays against various defenses and account for pass rushers who are going to pressure the quarterback, thereby increasing their chances for success.

We will begin with an in-depth look at three-step-drop pass protection schemes. Any team can develop an effective three-step-drop-passing attack and incorporate it into their offensive system as a complementary part of their basic offensive attack.

CONTENTS

Dedication _____ 3

Acknowledgements _____ 4

Chapter 1: What We Belive About Pass Protection _____ 7

Chapter 2: Three-Step Drop Protection _____ 12

Chapter 3: Five-Step Drop Protection _____ 32

Chapter 4: Play-Action Protection _____ 56

Chapter 5: Boot Action and Naked Protection _____ 73

Chapter 6: Sprint-Out Protection _____ 84

Chapter 7: Dash Protection _____ 106

Chapter 8: Putting It All Together _____ 116

About the Authors _____ 119

THREE-STEP
DROP PROTECTION

Every offensive unit in the country, regardless of the level at which they compete, or the particular offensive scheme which they emphasize, attempts to throw the quick out, the slant, and the fade in some way, shape, or form. For this reason, we think that any team can benefit from the development and implementation of sound three-step drop protection schemes. The majority of football coaches that utilize a quick passing package in some form or another, limit their offensive attacks by protecting every three-step drop pattern the same way, all of the time, versus every defensive front. By incorporating multiple protection schemes into their offensive attack, offensive coaches can vary their game plans to take advantage of the defensive personnel and weaknesses of their opponents on a week to week basis.

In general, most successful offensive football teams will have the confidence to utilize three-step drop patterns in virtually any down and distance situation as a normal and safe part of their offensive attack. When faced with aggressive defensive fronts that rely on getting to the quarterback with a variety of line movements, shifts, stunts, and blitzes, the efficient execution of an effective quick passing game becomes a necessity. Similarly, the ability to attack defenses with three-step drop patterns becomes more important when facing a shortened field in red zone situations. Because the quick passing game becomes most important when times are toughest, in situations that are likely to determine the outcome of games, it is imperative that the protection schemes used be basic and simple, as well as sound.

The strength of the three-step drop protection schemes that will be presented in this chapter is the fact that they are all sound AND easy to teach. These schemes do not require offensive players to do more than they are capable. The schemes discussed here are well thought out, have withstood the test of time, and lend themselves to a relatively seamless integration into any style of offensive attack.

Inside Gap Protection

The easiest three-step drop protection scheme to teach and to understand is the one used by the majority of high school football teams on Friday nights. In terms of responsibilities, inside gap protection is based on zone concepts and is very similar to extra point or field goal protection.

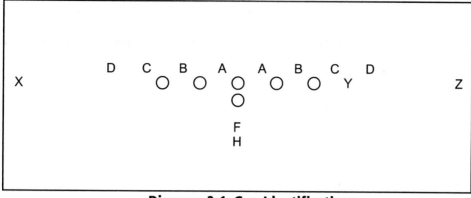

Diagram 2-1: Gap Identification

We identify the A, B, C, and D gaps to the right and to the left of the center. Each offensive lineman assigned to part of the protection scheme steps toward the center and blocks his inside gap. He keeps his shoulders parallel to the line of scrimmage and does not allow a defensive player to penetrate through his inside gap. As shown in Diagram 2-1, when we call a typical three-step drop pattern from I Right formation, the split end (X), tight end (Y), and flanker (Z) release immediately and run their respective routes.

The running backs are assigned a specific C gap to protect. In I formation, the full-back ALWAYS protects the short side of the formation because he is aligned closer to the line of scrimmage than the halfback. A pass rusher coming off of that edge of the formation will get to the quarterback faster than a pass rusher coming off of the edge from the tight end side of the formation. The running backs are told to run a path that splits the crotch of the offensive tackle's initial alignment, and are taught to "fit" on the edge by blocking the first wrong colored jersey that appears outside of the offensive tackle as he steps down toward the center to protect his inside gap. The running backs cannot ever widen their path to chase a defensive player who is lined up in the D gap. They must always step to and protect their C gap, forcing any defensive pass rusher to widen and come up the field outside of their block.

Diagrams 2-2 through 2-5 illustrate how the inside gap protection scheme varies based on the alignment of the running backs in four common two back formations. We have already mentioned that the fullback must protect the short side of the formation when he is aligned in an I formation. In the other two-back formations, the fullback is assigned to protect the C gap on his side of the formation.

While this protection scheme provides maximum protection in the A, B, and C gaps, the obvious shortcoming of the inside gap protection scheme is that only three receivers are ever allowed to release and become part of the pattern. We can use the inside gap protection scheme with any one-back formation to alter the alignment of the three receivers that will be involved in the pattern to take advantage of a particular defensive secondary coverage. As shown in Diagram 2-6, when we call a typical three-step drop pattern from Deuce Right formation, the halfback (H), split end (X), and flanker (Z) release immediately and run their respective routes.

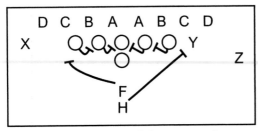

Diagram 2-2: I Right Formation

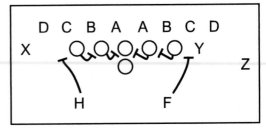

Diagram 2-3: Pro Right Formation

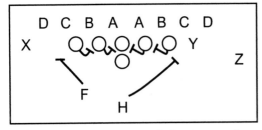

Diagram 2-4: Queen Right Formation

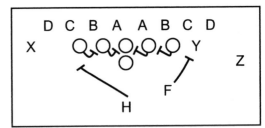

Diagram 2-5: King Right Formation

In most one-back formations, it is the fullback and the tight end who must protect the C gaps on their respective sides of the formation. The fullback is again told to run a path that splits the crotch of the offensive tackle's initial alignment, and is taught to "fit" on the edge by blocking the first wrong colored jersey to appear outside of the offensive tackle as he steps down toward the center to protect his inside gap. The fullback and tight end cannot ever widen out to chase a defensive player who is lined up in the D gap. They must always step to and protect their C gap, forcing any defensive pass rusher to widen and come up the field outside of their block.

Diagrams 2-7 through 2-10 illustrate how the inside-gap protection scheme varies based on the alignment of the tight end in four common one back formations. We do not think that we ever have to protect the D gap on either side of any formation when we call a three-step drop pattern. If the quarterback takes his three-step drop and delivers the ball in 1.5 seconds as he is taught, then no outside rusher will have time to pressure the throw. The biggest advantage of the inside-gap protection scheme is that we never have to worry about what defensive front we are trying to protect against. We simply empha-size the protection of all six inside gaps by the five offensive linemen and two running backs and insist that the quarterback deliver the ball in rhythm and on time.

Slide Gap Protection

Our favorite three-step drop protection scheme is also based upon zone concepts. While somewhat more involved than our inside-gap protection scheme, slide-gap protection still assigns an offensive player to each of the three inside gaps (A, B, and C), and dictates that a defensive pass rusher from the D gap will be allowed to come free. We will slide our gap protection scheme to the right with a Ram call, and to the left with a Lion call.

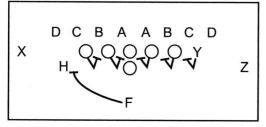

Diagram 2-6: Deuce Right Formation

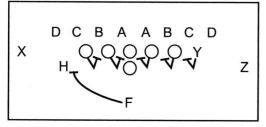

Diagram 2-7: Deuce Right Formation

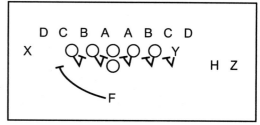

Diagram 2-8: Trey Right Formation

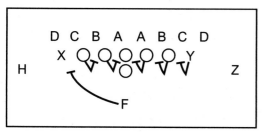

Diagram 2-9: Ace Right Formation

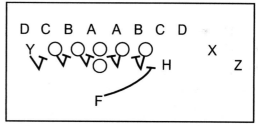

Diagram 2-10: Trips Left Formation

Our center will make the Ram or Lion call at the line of scrimmage based upon the structure of the defense that he sees, following some basic rules which we will discuss in a moment. For everyone else on the offensive line, slide-gap protection is no more diffi-cult to understand than inside-gap protection. They simply have to determine whether they are protecting their inside gap or their outside gap. In actuality, the center is going to tell them which way to go.

The primary advantage of our basic slide-gap protection scheme is the opportunity for offensive coaches to involve a fourth receiver, usually a running back, in the three-step drop pattern without sacrificing their ability to protect the quarterback. The running back that remains part of the protection scheme is still assigned to the C gap, exactly as he is in inside-gap protection. When involved in the slide-gap protection scheme, the

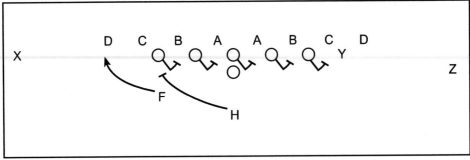

Diagram 2-11: Ram Call

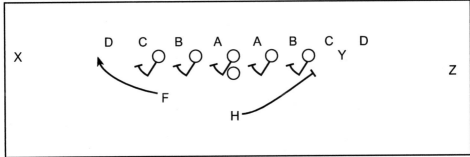

Diagram 2-12: Lion Call

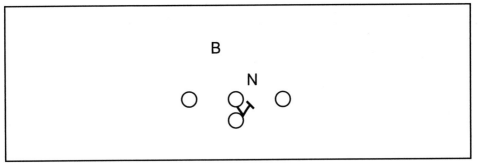

Diagram 2-13: Defender in the Call Side A Gap (Ram)

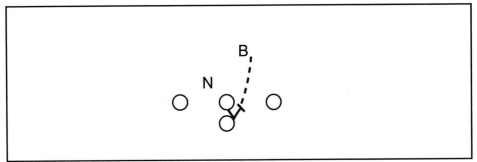

Diagram 2-14: Defender in the Backside A Gap (Ram)

running back always protects the C gap AWAY from where we are sliding our protection. On a Ram call, the running back would protect the left C gap, and on a Lion call, he would protect the right C gap.

Diagram 2-11 illustrates the slide-gap, three-step drop protection scheme when our center makes a Ram call. The fullback (F), split end (X), tight end (Y), and flanker (Z) release immediately and run their respective routes. We slide the protection scheme to the right and tell the halfback to protect the left C gap.

Diagram 2-12 illustrates the slide-gap, three-step drop protection scheme when our center makes a Lion call. The fullback (F), split end (X), tight end (Y), and flanker (Z) release immediately and run their respective routes. We slide the protection scheme to the right and tell the halfback to work opposite of the call and protect the right C gap.

Because we are now protecting all six inside gaps with the five offensive linemen and only one running back, we can now get an extra receiver out into a route. Obviously, this alignment gives us a better opportunity to take advantage of the vulnerable areas in an opponent's underneath coverage. For this reason alone, we prefer slide-gap protection to inside-gap protection. We still insist that the quarterback deliver the ball in rhythm and on time. As long as the quarterback takes his three-step drop and delivers the ball in 1.5 seconds as he is taught, then no outside rusher will have time to pressure the throw.

Each player's individual technique in the slide-gap protection scheme is somewhat more complex than it was in the inside-gap protection scheme. We will begin a more detailed discussion of each player's assignment by examining the center's responsibilities.

If the center makes a Ram call and a defensive player is aligned in the A gap to his right, then the center simply drops his right foot four to six inches and attacks the defensive player in his assigned A gap. A Ram call tells the center to block the A gap to his right. When there is a defensive player aligned in that gap, his assignment should be rather obvious.

Sometimes the center will make a Ram call and there will NOT be a defensive player aligned in the A gap to his right, but there will be a defensive player aligned in the A gap to his left. In this situation, with no immediate threat in his assigned A gap, the center will again drop his right foot four to six inches and help the left guard by using his left arm to punch the A gap defender in order to blunt his attack. While doing this, the center must focus his attention on the second level and be aware of a linebacker that may try to run through his assigned right A gap. The Ram call still tells the center to block the A gap to his right. When there is no defensive player aligned in that gap, he is able to help the left guard while still carrying out his own assignment by looking for a blitz through his assigned gap.

When the center makes a Ram call and has a defender playing him head up, the center will treat that defender exactly the same way as a defender lined up in either A gap. If the head up player slants to the call side, he then becomes a right A gap defender,

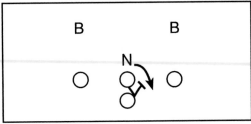

Diagram 2-15: Defender in a 0 Technique Slanting Right (Ram)

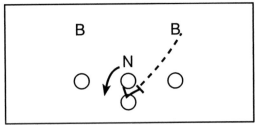

Diagram 2-16: Defender in a 0 Technique Slanting Left (Ram)

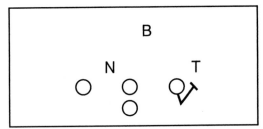

Diagram 2-17: Call Side 3 or 4i Technique (Ram)

and the center simply drops his right foot four to six inches and attacks him. Again, the Ram call tells the center to block the A gap to his right, and when the defensive player slants toward that gap, the center's assignment is to block him.

If the head-up player slants away from the call side, he becomes a left A gap defender on a Ram call. In this situation, with no immediate threat in his assigned A gap, the center will again drop his right foot four to six inches and help the left guard by using his left arm to punch the slanting defender in order to blunt his attack. While doing this, the center must focus his attention on the second level, and be aware of a linebacker that may try to run through his assigned right A gap.

Let's consider the guard's assignment next. When the center makes a Ram call, the right guard knows that he has to drop his right foot four to six inches on a 45-degree angle and protect the B gap. If there is a defensive player in his assigned gap, he must attack him, as shown in Diagram 2-17.

If the center makes a Ram call and a defensive player is not aligned in the B gap, but there is a defensive player aligned in the A gap to the inside of the right guard, then the

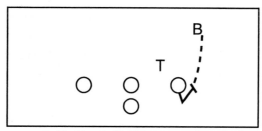

Diagram 2-18: No Call Side 3 Or 4i Technique (Ram)

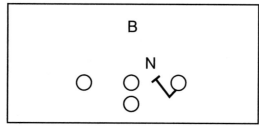

Diagram 2-19: Call Side Shade or 2i Technique (Lion)

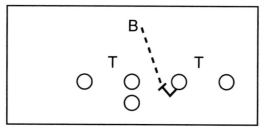

Diagram 2-20: No Call Side Shade or 2i Technique (Lion)

right guard will again drop his right foot four to six inches and help the center by using his left arm to chip the defender lined up in the A gap in order to blunt his attack. While doing this, the right guard must focus his eyes on the second level and look for a linebacker that may try to run through the B gap. The Ram call tells the guard to block the B gap to his right. When there is no defensive player aligned in that gap, he is able to help the center while still carrying out his own assignment by looking for a blitz through his assigned gap as shown in Diagram 2-18.

If the center makes a Lion call, the right guard knows that he has to drop his left foot four to six inches on a 45-degree angle and protect the A gap. If there is a defensive player in his assigned gap, he must attack him, as shown in Diagram 2-19.

If the center makes a Lion call and a defensive player is not aligned in the A gap, then the right guard will again drop his left foot four to six inches and help the right tackle by using his right arm to chip the defender lined up in the B gap in order to blunt his attack. While doing this, the right guard must focus his eyes on the second level and look for a linebacker that may try to run through the right A gap. The Lion call tells the right guard

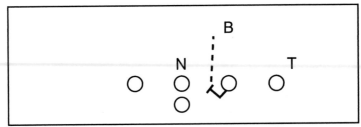

Diagram 2-21: Uncovered Guard (Lion)

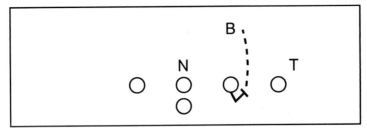

Diagram 2-22: Uncovered Guard (Ram)

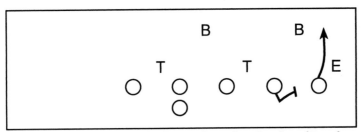

Diagram 2-23: Cut Block on the Edge Rusher (Ram)

to block the A gap to his left. When there is no defensive player aligned in that gap, he is able to help the right tackle while still carrying out his own assignment by looking for a blitz through his assigned gap as shown in Diagram 2-20.

In some situations, the right guard will be completely uncovered. There will not be a defender lined up in either the A or B gap to his side of the formation. As shown in Diagrams 2-21 and 2-22, the right guard will take his proper drop step and look to the second level for a linebacker that may try to run through his assigned gap.

While the responsibility of the offensive tackle is similar to that of the center and the guard, we teach him to use a slightly different technique in accomplishing his task. The tackle is taught to take a proper drop step with his call-side foot just like the other linemen, but we vary his technique by asking him to attempt to cut block the defensive pass rusher threatening the C gap whenever possible. We do this because we want to force the outside pass rusher coming off of the edge to keep his hands down. Obviously, pass patterns designed in conjunction with three-step drop protection schemes usually emphasize quick throws by the quarterback delivered to the perimeter of the field. We

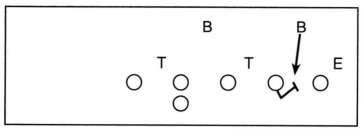

Diagram 2-24: Protecting Against a C Gap Blitz (Ram)

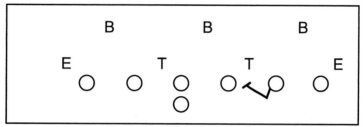

Diagram 2-25: Call Side 3 or 4i Technique (Lion)

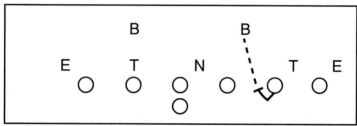

Diagram 2-26: No Call Side 3 or 4i Technique (Lion)

want to get the hands of the widest pass rushers down so that they cannot bat or knock passes down before they cross the line of scrimmage.

In Diagram 2-23, we see a situation in which we expect the right tackle to take a four-to-six inch drop step with his right foot at a 45-degree angle and protect his C gap responsibility by attempting to cut block the defensive end who is going to pass rush off of the edge of the formation.

In Diagram 2-24, the same defensive structure now forces us to handle a C gap blitz. In this situation, we again teach the right tackle to take a four-to-six inch drop step with his right foot at a 45-degree angle and protect his C gap responsibility. In this case, the tackle is more likely to attack the blitzing linebacker than to attempt to cut him. We will not normally try to cut block an interior pass rusher when there is an additional defender coming off of the edge to his outside.

Remember that we are not going to protect the D gap to either side of any formation when we call a three-step drop pattern. In slide-gap protection, we are going to protect all six inside gaps with five offensive linemen and one running back. We will protect the

C gaps and allow defenders to pass rush through the D gaps and come free. When an offensive tackle is on the tight-end side of a formation, he must focus on his gap assignment and ignore any pass rusher aligned over the tight end who is going to release into the pattern and run a route.

As shown in Diagram 2-25, if the center makes a Lion call and the right tackle has a B gap responsibility, then the tackle is going to drop his left foot four to six inches on a 45-degree angle and protect the B gap. When there is a down lineman in his assigned gap, the tackle can be extremely aggressive in attacking that defensive B gap player, using a technique that will look exactly the same as a down block in our run game.

In Diagram 2-26, the center makes a Lion call and the right tackle does NOT have a defender aligned in the B gap. With no immediate threat in the B gap, the tackle will take a four-to-six inch drop step with his left foot and help the running back by using his right arm to punch the C gap defender in order to blunt his attack. While doing this, the tackle must focus his attention on the second level and be aware of a linebacker trying to run through the B gap. The Lion call tells the tackle to block the B gap. When there is no defensive player aligned in that gap, he is able to help the running back while still carrying out his own assignment by looking for a blitz through the B gap.

We have already said that a running back will always protect the C gap AWAY from where we are sliding our protection. On a Ram call, a running back will protect the left C gap, and on a Lion call, he will protect the right C gap. The running back's responsibility is similar to that of the offensive tackle in that we teach him to attempt to cut block the defensive pass rusher threatening the C gap whenever possible. This action forces the outside pass rusher to keep his hands down so that he cannot bat or knock passes down before they cross the line of scrimmage.

We have already mentioned that we like our basic slide-gap protection scheme because it allows us to get a fourth receiver out into the three-step drop pattern without sacrificing our ability to protect the quarterback. Because we are sound in our protection of all six inside gaps with only six offensive players (the five offensive linemen and one running back), we can utilize our slide-gap protection scheme from a wide variety of formations.

The ability to involve a fourth receiver in the pattern gives us a much better chance to take advantage of the vulnerable areas in an opponent's underneath coverage, and capitalize upon the weaknesses inherent in the structure of any defense. Because the tight end is never involved in our slide-gap pass protection scheme, we can vary our personnel and use a variety of no tight-end formations as well.

By making one slight adjustment in the basic slide-gap protection scheme, we can safely utilize our three-step passing attack in conjunction with no-back formations against certain defensive fronts. The offensive tackle on the back side of the directional Ram or Lion call must protect the edge pass rusher rather than protect his call-side gap.

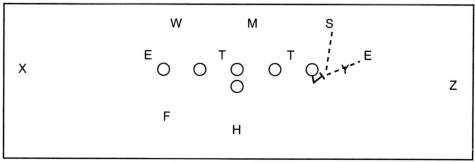

Diagram 2-27: Ram Call

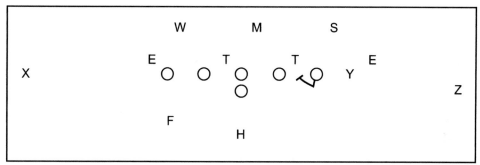

Diagram 2-28: Lion Call

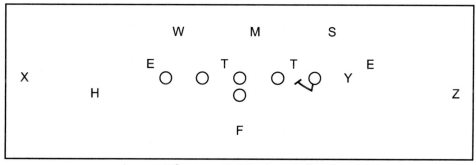

Diagram 2-29: Lion Call

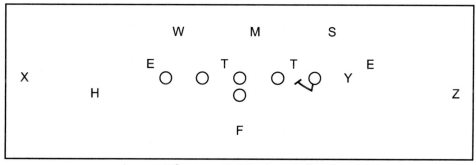

Diagram 2-30: Lion Call

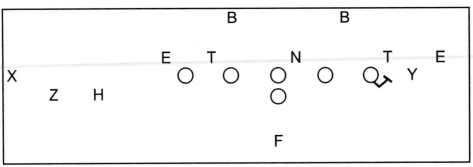

Diagram 2-31: Ram Call

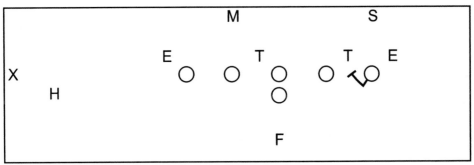

Diagram 2-32: Lion Call

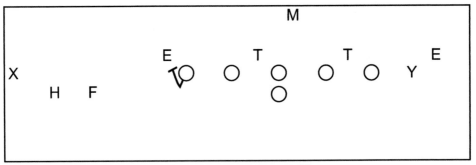

Diagram 2-33: Ram Call

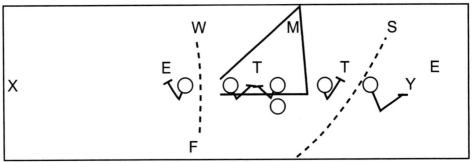

Diagram 2-34: Man Protection

In Diagram 2-33, the left tackle would not block the B gap as he does in normal situations. With an empty backfield, he has to stay on the C gap edge pass rusher. We cannot use our three-step passing attack from no-back formations unless we are certain that the opponent that we are facing will alter the structure of his defense by removing a second-level player (linebacker) from the tight end to the tackle box in order to defend the receivers. If the defense does not take players out of the tight end to tackle box to defend the additional receivers, then the slide-gap protection scheme is going to be unsound to the side of the formation away from the directional call. We do not think that the risk of exposing our quarterback will be offset by the potential reward of an uncovered receiver.

Man Protection

A third protection scheme that teams can use to protect their three-step drop quick passing attack relies upon man concepts. From a philosophical perspective, the man-protection scheme is very similar to the inside-gap protection scheme in that it 1) is a very basic and effective way to protect the quarterback, and 2) involves five offensive linemen and two running backs in the protection scheme. While this protection scheme also provides sound protection in most situations, it allows the running backs to become involved in the pattern if the man to whom they are assigned drops into coverage rather than rushing the passer.

Diagram 2-34 shows the basic man-protection scheme versus a standard defense. The theory behind the man-protection scheme is that the offensive unit will always block the biggest and most physical pass rushers (the defensive down linemen) with the biggest and most physical blockers (the offensive linemen). By using a man-protection scheme, we can eliminate the need for a running back to have to try and block a down lineman who is coming free off of the edge of the structure of the defense. It also enables us to block the fastest and most athletic pass rushers (linebackers and defensive backs) with our fastest and most athletic blockers (the running backs). It is the personnel of an opponent, rather than the defensive scheme that the defense plays, that would cause us to consider using a man protection scheme. Diagrams 2-35 through 2-37 show the man-protection scheme versus some other common defensive fronts.

In the man-protection scheme, the offensive linemen are able to be very aggressive in their pass-protection technique. Against most defenses, the center will have help from one of the guards, who will be uncovered. The center and the guard will utilize a double-team technique in which the center will usually read and come off to a second-level player (linebacker) as shown in Diagram 2-38.

In order for the quick-passing attack to be most effective, we must be able to release the running backs into the pattern when the defense is not bringing extra pass rushers from the second level. The man-protection scheme allows us to do this by assigning the running backs to a read-protection technique. If the linebacker rushes the passer, then

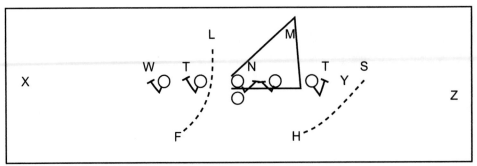

Diagram 2-35: Reduced Defense

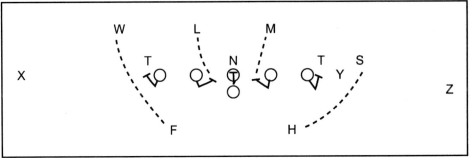

Diagram 2-36: Okie Defense

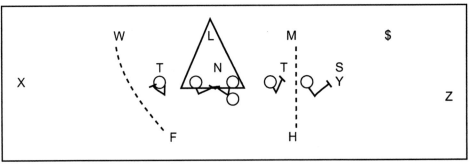

Diagram 2-37: Slide Weak Defense

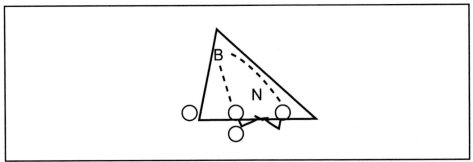

Diagram 2-38: Double Team Off to Linebacker

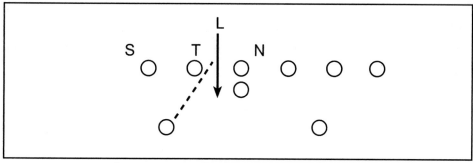

Diagram 2-39: Linebacker Shooting a Gap

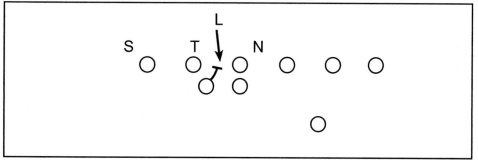

Diagram 2-40: Adjustment to Crowded Linebacker

the assigned running back must pick him up. When the linebacker drops into coverage, the running back will release into the pattern and run a route that complements the pattern being run.

The man-protection scheme must be able to account for situations in which a linebacker crowds the line of scrimmage, anticipates the snap count, and attempts to come free through a gap after the offensive linemen are set in their stances. This problem is shown in Diagram 2-39. We cannot expect the back to pick up the linebacker from his normal alignment.

A common solution to this problem is shown in Diagram 2-40. By simply teaching the running back to cheat his alignment up as soon as the linebacker shows his blitz, we do not have to alter the basic man-protection scheme in any way. Obviously, this tips the defense off to our intention to throw the ball, but it is the easiest way to account for the blitz.

Another situation that the man-protection scheme must be able to handle is the problem presented by defenses that rely upon moving and slanting their down linemen a majority of the time. Diagram 2-41 illustrates the problem. Because the offensive linemen will not get any help in the man-protection scheme, they must become effective in their pass-protection techniques.

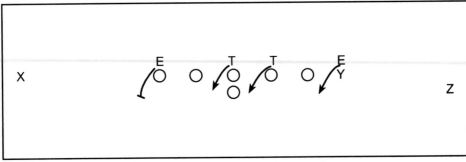

Diagram 2-41: Angle or Slant Defense

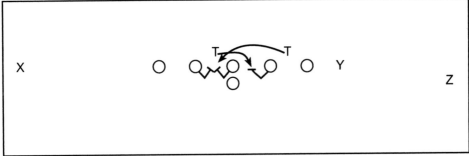

Diagram 2-42: Interior Twist

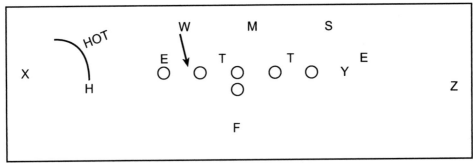

Diagram 2-43: Hot Read on Will Linebacker

Similarly, offensive coaches who utilize the man-protection scheme must be able to account for a variety of line stunts and twists. By incorporating some zone concepts into the basic scheme, most of these movements can be dealt with effectively. Diagram 2-42 shows how a basic line twist can be handled by zoning the stunt off between the adjacent offensive linemen.

The man-protection scheme is safe because the responsibilities and blocking assignments are obvious to everyone on the field and the sidelines. There is never any uncertainty about who is responsible to pick up and block any pass rusher. The coach must ultimately be held responsible for preparing his team to face a given opponent. The offensive unit must be able to identify every defensive front that they are going to see and understand where the second level players like to blitz.

The only way to utilize man-protection schemes in conjunction with one-back formations is to incorporate a series of hot reads. The one-back formation takes a protector out of the backfield and turns him into a receiver. This alignement means that all potential pass rushers can no longer be accounted for should they blitz. Recall that we began with the premise that throwing it hot is never a good answer. Nonetheless, if we are determined to attack defenses with a three-step drop quick passing attack and want to line up in one-back formations, we can still utilize man-protection schemes if we are willing to force our quarterback to make hot reads. In these situations we will we will specify exactly who the defender is that we cannot account for, and instruct the quarterback where to throw the ball if he rushes. Quite simply, the quarterback must throw the ball before the unaccounted for pass rusher can get to him.

In Diagram 2-43, the one-back formation shows that the Will linebacker can no longer be blocked by the halfback (H) who is now in the slot. If the Will linebacker blitzes, the quarterback must deliver the ball to the halfback (H) in the flat. It is imperative that we build hot reads and routes into the three-step drop patterns if we indeed intend to use man-protection schemes with one-back and no-back formations.

Maximum Protection

Ever since the Chicago Bears dominated the National Football League in 1985 with Buddy Ryan's version of the 46 defense, some defensive coordinators have chosen to play some form of attack, blitz, or charge front. These situations are predicated upon taking risks and sacrificing the coverage of secondary receivers in certain situations in order to put pressure on, and get to, the quarterback. Any offensive coach who wants to throw the ball needs to have a way to handle defenses that are going to consistently bring more pass rushers than can be accounted for.

Regardless of how we choose to protect our three-step drop quick passing attack, the use of maximum protection allows us to throw the three-step drop patterns against eight- and nine-man fronts. Maximum protection simply means that we are going to keep the tight end and both running backs in to protect the quarterback, and run only a basic two-receiver pattern.

Diagrams 2-44 through 2-46 illustrate ways to use maximum protection with inside-gap protection, slide-gap protection, and man protection. Notice that in this situation, we ARE protecting the D gap in our zone-protection schemes.

Any coach who wants to throw the ball should always have a plan to account for this type of sustained defensive pressure that will overwhelm any normal type of pass protection.

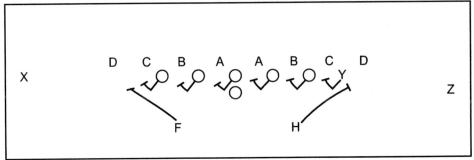

Diagram 2-44: Maximum Inside Gap Protection

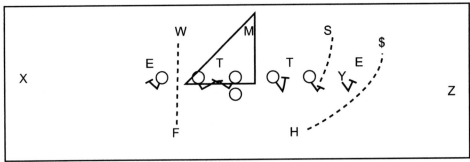

Diagram 2-45: Maximum Slide Gap Protection (Lion)

Diagram 2-46: Maximum Man Protection

Summary

We have presented several ways to protect the quick-passing attack. It is important to determine which protection scheme or schemes best fits each style of offensive attack. Among the factors to consider are the following:

How often will I utilize the three-step passing attack? Coaches who are going to throw the quick pass two or three times in a game will be able to use a much more basic scheme than coaches who are going to throw the quick pass ten or fifteen times in a game.

How much practice time can I afford to devote to pass protection? It does not make any sense to use thirty minutes of valuable practice time every day to work on an aspect of the offensive game plan that might be run a maximum of five times in an actual game. Teams with more extensive quick passing attacks need to spend more time examining how to protect those plays.

Which protection scheme is most readily tied to our basic offensive attack? What a team does when they run the ball should be closely related to what they do when they throw the ball. Offensive linemen will have more success if what they are asked to do in both situations does not radically change.

How will we teach our offensive line and how much can they pick up? Coaches must teach whatever protection scheme in which they believe. They must understand it well enough to teach it to their players. Even football teams that intend to throw the football often cannot afford to use multiple protection schemes if their offensive linemen are not able to differentiate between the schemes, and implement them correctly against the defensive fronts that they are going to face.

Have I kept my basic protection scheme as simple as I can? The best protection schemes have clearly defined rules and give all players specific responsibilities. As a general rule, the more players can react to what they see without thinking about it, the more effective the protection will be.

CHAPTER 3

FIVE-STEP
DROP PROTECTION

The five-step drop pass protection schemes that can be utilized to keep pass rushers away from the quarterback include man-blocking schemes, zone-blocking schemes, and blocking schemes that combine some aspects of both. All of these five-step drop pass-protection schemes are designed to time up with pass patterns that attack the intermediate and deep zones in the defensive secondary.

Man Protection

A man-protection scheme is the most basic five-step drop pass-protection scheme available to offensive coaches. In man pass-protection schemes, the offensive linemen and the running backs are assigned to block specific defensive players. Diagram 3-1 shows how a man-blocking scheme can be used to protect the quarterback in an offensive system utilizing a five-step drop passing attack.

This type of pass-protection scheme allows the split end (X), tight end (Y), and flanker (Z) to release into the pattern immediately. Each running back is assigned a specific linebacker to block. If that linebacker becomes a pass rusher, then the running back is responsible for blocking him. If that linebacker drops into coverage, then the running back is coached to release and run an underneath pass route that will complement the routes being run by the other receivers involved in the pattern. These pass routes are called check routes because a running back must check to see what his linebacker is doing on the snap of the ball, before he can release and run his assigned route.

This responsibility is known as a check-release, telling the running back to check his assigned linebacker and release if he drops into coverage. These check routes are designed to complement the routes being run by receivers X, Y, and Z, who are releasing into the pattern immediately. Diagrams 3-2, 3-3, and 3-4 show three commonly used check routes. While several possible check routes exist, these diagrams illustrate how the underneath routes can complement the other routes being run as part of the pattern.

Diagram 3-5 shows a man-protection scheme used to protect a five-step drop pattern run against a defense aligned in a Slide Weak front.

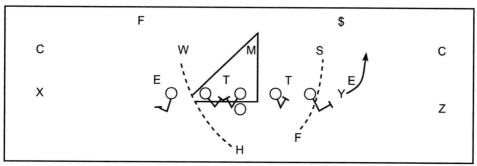

Diagram 3-1: Man Protection Scheme

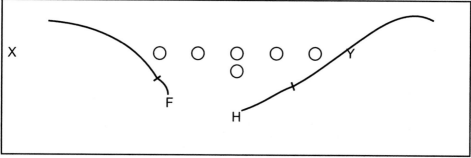

Diagram 3-2: Check Flat Route

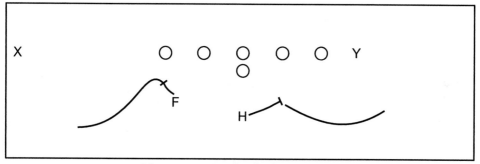

Diagram 3-3: Check Flare Route

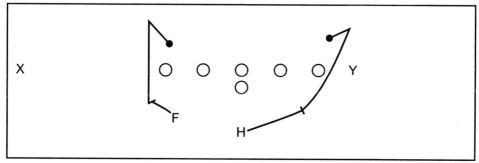

Diagram 3-4: Check Stop Route

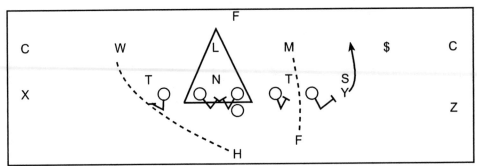

Diagram 3-5: Man Protection vs. Slide Weak Front

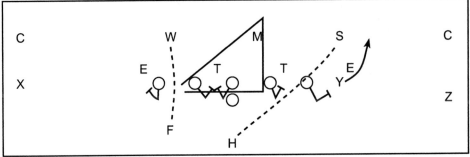

Diagram 3-6: Shaded Nose Guard

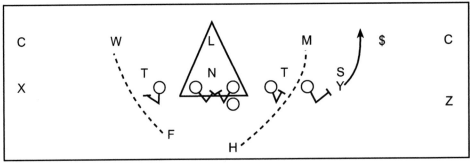

Diagram 3-7: Stacked Linebacker

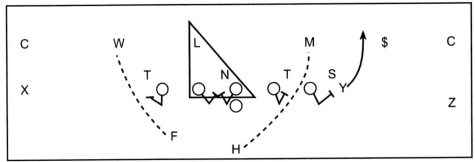

Diagram 3-8: Shaded Nose Guard

The structure of Slide Weak includes a stacked inside linebacker as part of the defensive front. In the man pass-protection scheme, if an offensive lineman is covered (i.e., a defensive player is aligned over him on the line of scrimmage), then the offensive lineman is responsible for blocking that defensive player. If the structure of the defense includes a stacked inside linebacker, or a shaded defensive lineman, then the protection scheme needs to be able to account for the stacked or shaded player(s). Making two adjacent offensive linemen responsible for both a down lineman and a second-level player (linebacker or defensive back) solves this problem. This technique is illustrated in the diagrams by drawing a triangle around the two defensive players that the offensive linemen are responsible for. Diagrams 3-6 through 3-8 show three defensive fronts that require the use of this technique.

In these examples, the two offensive linemen utilize a zone concept, blocking the down lineman while keeping their eyes focused on the linebacker. If the linebacker becomes a pass rusher, then one of the offensive linemen must come off of the double-team to block the blitzing linebacker. If the linebacker drops into coverage and never rushes the passer, then both offensive linemen continue to double-team the down lineman.

The most difficult and time consuming aspect of incorporating the man pass-protection scheme into an offensive system is making certain that every offensive player with a potential pass-protection responsibility recognizes every defensive front that he will face in the course of a game or season. Obviously, it is the responsibility of the offensive coaching staff to prepare players to recognize every defensive front that an opponent is liable to play. Defensive units that are multiple in their alignments and vary their gap responsibilities become harder to prepare for than those who line up in a base front the majority of the time.

Diagram 3-9 shows how the man-protection scheme can be used to protect a five-step drop pass pattern against a Strong Eagle defensive front, while Diagram 3-10 shows how the man-protection scheme can be used to protect a five-step drop pass pattern against an Okie defensive front.

Out Protection

It is possible to vary the man-protection scheme against defensive units that like to play an Okie front the majority of the time. Diagram 3-11 shows Out protection used to protect a five-step drop pass pattern against an Okie defensive front.

It is important to consider what kind of release is best for the running back to take in order to run his check route. If the running back is assigned to check-release and run a flat route (Diagram 3-2), then Out protection is less effective because the running back has to step up and check the inside linebacker before releasing outside to the flat. Out protection is much more compatible with a check-stop route (Diagram 3-4) which dictates that the running back should end up in the middle of the field, where his protection responsibility is initially aligned.

The primary advantages of the man-protection scheme are in its simplicity, and the fact that it can be used against any defensive front to prevent pass rushers from coming free and unblocked toward the quarterback. It is important that the limitations of the man pass-protection scheme are understood before it is incorporated into any offensive system.

It is possible that the running backs may never get released into their check routes against defenses that align in odd-man fronts. These defenses will force the offense to assign seven players to the pass-protection scheme even in situations where only five defensive players are rushing the passer. With no underneath routes to worry about, this allows the defensive secondary to squeeze the intermediate routes, thereby narrowing the passing lanes. This problem is shown in Diagram 3-12.

In Diagram 3-12, the running backs are assigned to the outside linebackers—both of whom are rushing the passer. While only five defenders are rushing the passer, the offensive guards are wasted since seven offensive players are kept in to protect against only five pass rushers.

Diagram 3-13 shows the same problem resulting from the use of Out protection. In this case, the running backs are assigned to the inside linebackers—both of whom are rushing the passer. Again, only five defenders are rushing the passer. Similarly, the offensive tackles are wasted since seven offensive players are kept in to protect against only five pass rushers.

Another disadvantage of the man-protection scheme is that no effective way exists to deal with defenses that like to rush eight defenders. The man protection scheme involves a maximum of seven offensive players in the protection scheme. If the defense decides to rush an eighth player, the offense has no way to account for him. The eighth pass rusher will always come free against the man-protection scheme. This is the worst situation for a pass-oriented offensive unit to be in. An example of this problem is shown in Diagram 3-14. If the strong safety blitzes, there is no way to account for him.

Scat Protection

Offenses can deal with this problem by utilizing a Scat scheme to assign one of the running backs to account for two potential pass rushers. The running back will block whichever player becomes a pass rusher by blocking the inside pass rusher and allowing the outside pass rusher to come free if both players rush. Diagram 3-15 shows the Scat scheme. The Scat scheme can also be used along with Out protection as shown in Diagram 3-16.

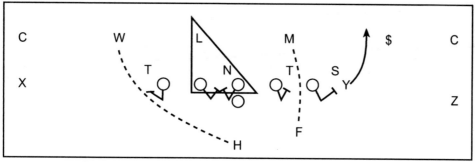

Diagram 3-9: Man Protection vs. Strong Eagle Front

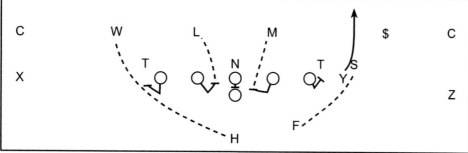

Diagram 3-10: Man Protection vs. Okie Front

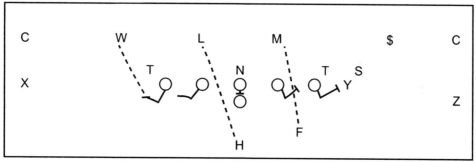

Diagram 3-11: Out Protection vs. Okie

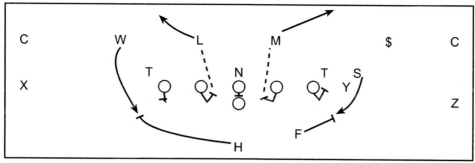

Diagram 3-12: Man Protection vs. Okie Front

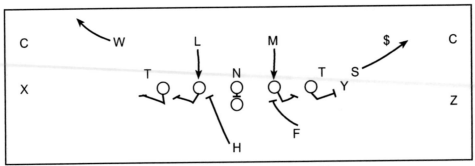

Diagram 3-13: Out Protection vs. Okie Front

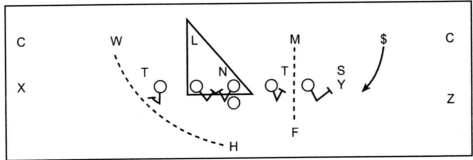

Diagram 3-14: Strong Safety Blitz

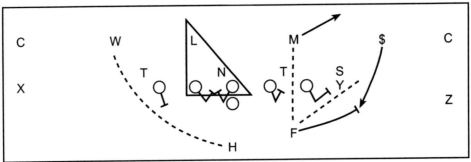

Diagram 3-15: Strong Eagle Defense

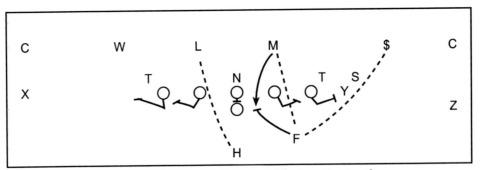

Diagram 3-16: Scat Scheme with Out Protection

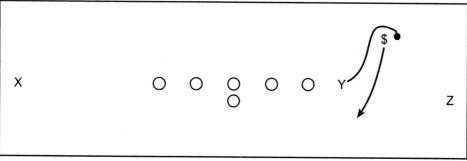

Diagram 3-17: Hot Route Versus Zone Coverage

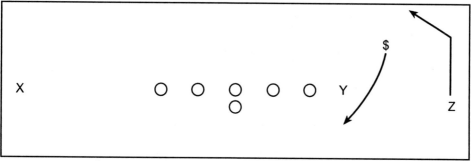

Diagram 3-18: Hot Route Versus Man Coverage

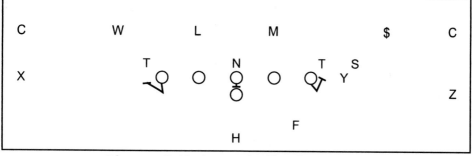

Diagram 3-19: Covered Offensive Tackles

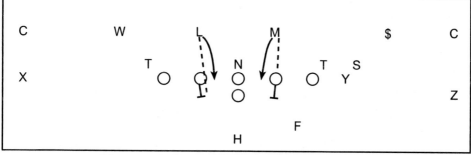

Diagram 3-20: Uncovered Offensive Guards

The problem can also be dealt with by making the quarterback responsible for the eighth pass rusher. However, we will not do this unless we have eliminated all other alternatives as viable options. In those situations, we are forced to make the quarterback recognize which pass rusher we cannot account for, and utilize a hot read to deal with that defender. This adjustment could involve an audible at the line of scrimmage that changes the called play to a three-step drop quick pass, or the receiver might be coached to automatically adjust his route when the eighth pass rusher does blitz the quarterback. In either case, the quarterback has to identify the defender that we cannot protect, and realize where he has to deliver the football if that player does blitz. Examples of hot reads are shown in Diagrams 3-17 and 3-18, against both zone and man coverage.

This adjustment requires a great deal of emphasis and time in practice to make sure that the quarterback and the receivers are on the same page. Both players have to 1) understand which type of protection scheme is being utilized, 2) identify the structure of the defense, 3) note the alignment of the potential eighth rusher, and 4) know what route adjustments will be made if that player does blitz.

Double-Read Protection

In order to give ourselves a better opportunity to take advantage of the coverage that the defensive secondary is playing, we can incorporate a Double Read into our pass protection scheme. The Double Read technique allows us to account for seven potential pass rushers with only five offensive players, and get the running backs involved in the pattern on a consistent basis.

The Double Read scheme is similar to the man pass-protection scheme in that any covered offensive lineman must block the defender that is aligned over him on the line of scrimmage. This part of the Double Read scheme is shown in Diagram 3-19.

The uncovered offensive linemen and the running backs actually make the Double Read. An uncovered offensive lineman reads the inside linebacker who is aligned over him. If the inside linebacker blitzes, then the uncovered offensive lineman must block him as shown in Diagram 3-20.

The running back, on the same side of the formation as the uncovered offensive lineman, also reads the inside linebacker over that offensive lineman. If the inside linebacker blitzes, then the running back knows that the offensive lineman is going to block him. He then immediately switches his read to the outside linebacker on that side of the formation. This action is shown in Diagram 3-21.

The term Double Read derives its name from the uncovered offensive lineman and the running back both reading the same defensive player. If the inside linebacker drops into pass coverage instead of blitzing, then the uncovered lineman switches his read to the outside linebacker on that side of the formation. If the outside linebacker blitzes, then the uncovered offensive lineman must block him as shown in Diagram 3-22.

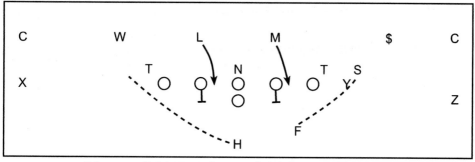

Diagram 3-21: Running Back In The Double Read

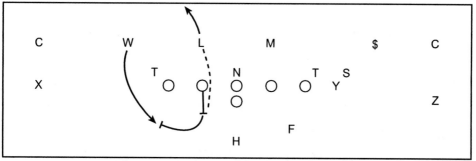

Diagram 3-22: Outside Linebacker Blitz

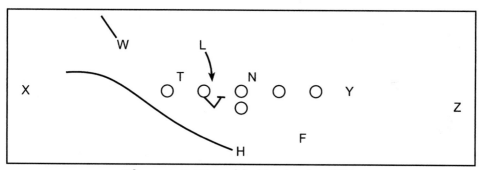

Diagram 3-23: Inside Linebacker Blitz

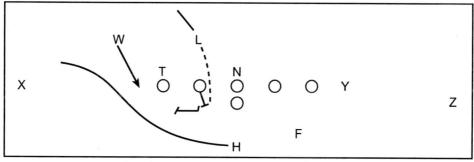

Diagram 3-24: Outside Linebacker Blitz

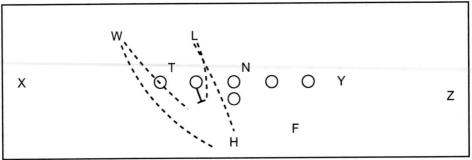

Diagram 3-25: Inside Linebacker Blitz

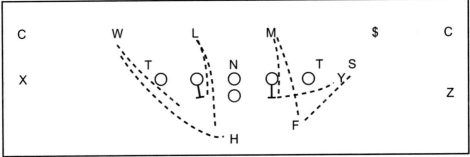

Diagram 3-26: Double Read vs. Okie Front

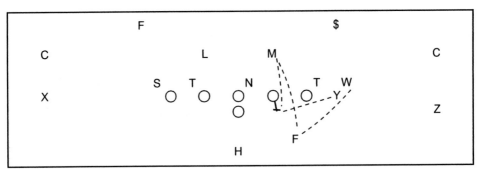

Diagram 3-27: Double-Read vs. Reduced Front

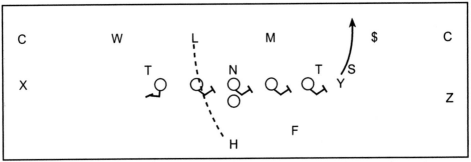

Diagram 3-28: Slide Right Zone Scheme

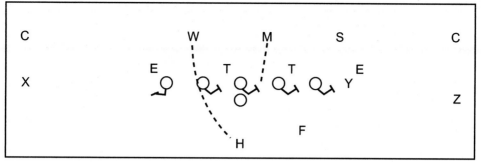

Diagram 3-29: Zone Scheme vs. 4-3 Front

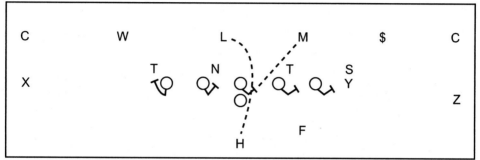

Diagram 3-30: Zone Scheme vs. Slide Weak Front

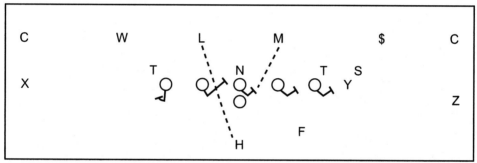

Diagram 3-31: Zone Scheme vs. Okie Front

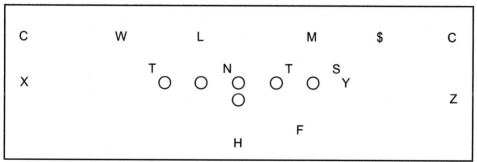

Diagram 3-32: Zone Scheme vs. Strong Eagle Front

We have already noted that the running back on the same side of the formation as the uncovered offensive lineman also reads the inside linebacker over that offensive lineman. If the inside linebacker drops into pass coverage instead of blitzing, then the running back knows that he can release into the pattern because the uncovered offensive lineman is now going to switch his read to the outside linebacker on that side of the formation. As shown in Diagrams 3-23 and 3-24, the running back can safely release into the pattern whenever one of the linebackers blitzes. If both linebackers blitz, then the running back will not release into the pattern as shown in Diagram 3-25.

The Double-Read scheme gives the offense an opportunity to get the maximum number of receivers out into the pattern whenever the defense is trying to control the release of the running backs with an inside or outside blitz. The Double-Read scheme can only be used against defensive fronts that leave one or both of the offensive guards uncovered. Diagrams 3-26 and 3-27 illustrate two such fronts.

We can also utilize a zone scheme to protect five-step drop pass patterns. We employ our zone pass-protection scheme by building a directional call into the play, making a directional call either in the huddle or at the line of scrimmage. The first uncovered lineman away from the directional call will start a slide technique which will zone protect every gap. A right directional call is shown in Diagram 3-30.

This type of zone protection scheme allows the offensive linemen to know where help will come from and allows them to be more aggressive. It allows us to protect all four gaps to the side of the directional call. Diagrams 3-31 through 3-34 show the zone scheme used against a variety of defensive fronts.

We would utilize this type of zone pass protection scheme against defenses that try to create pressure by bringing four pass rushers to the strongside of the offensive formation. This adjustment provides effective pass protection to the strongside of the formation.

One Back Protection Schemes

The biggest factor in selecting a pass-protection scheme is how many receivers are going to be free released into the pattern without concern for a protection responsibility. Thus far, we have considered five-step drop pass patterns run from two-back formations. At this point, we will discuss the pass-protection schemes that we utilize with our one-back formations.

We employ the pass-protection concepts that we have already discussed when we want to throw the ball from one-back formations. The basic schemes that we use in two-back sets are at the heart of what we do from one-back formations. The remaining running back has exactly the same assignment, but will always be working opposite the tight end, who is now involved in the protection scheme. Diagram 3-33 shows our basic one-back protection.

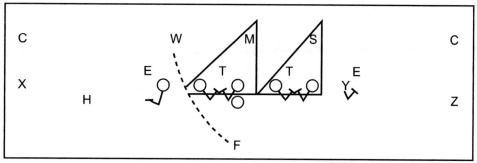

Diagram 3-33: One-Back Protection

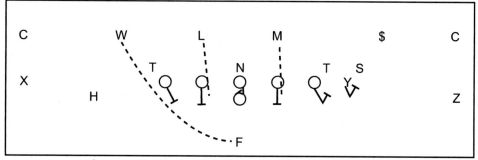

Diagram 3-34: One-Back Protection vs. Okie Front

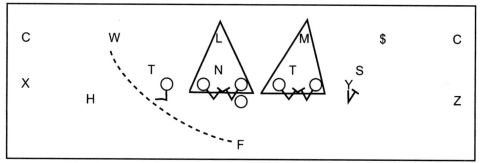

Diagram 3-35: One-Back Protection vs. Slide Weak Front

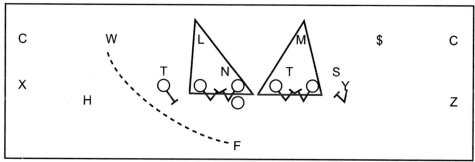

Diagram 3-36: One-Back Protection vs. 4-3 Front

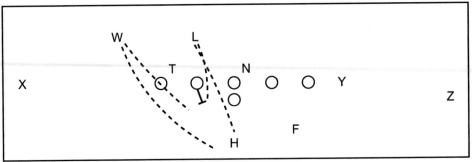

Diagram 3-25: Inside Linebacker Blitz

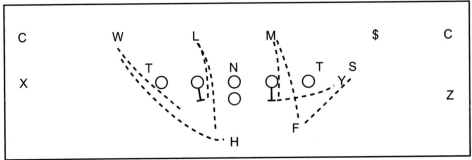

Diagram 3-26: Double Read vs. Okie Front

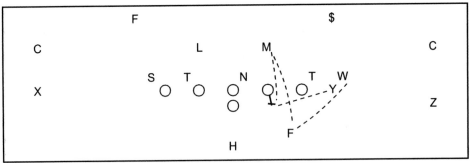

Diagram 3-27: Double Read vs. Reduced Front

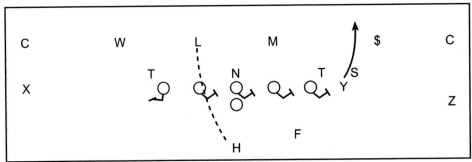

Diagram 3-28: Slide Right Zone Scheme

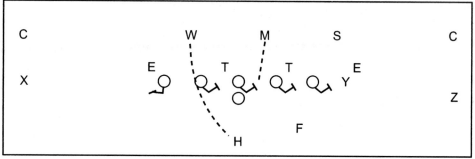

Diagram 3-37: Trips Right Formation

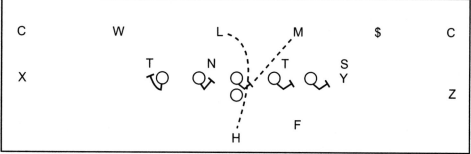

Diagram 3-38: Trey Right Formation

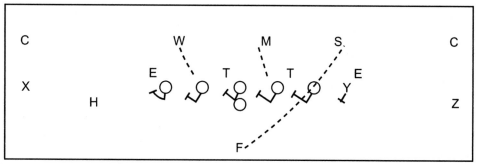

Diagram 3-39: One-Back Zone Protection

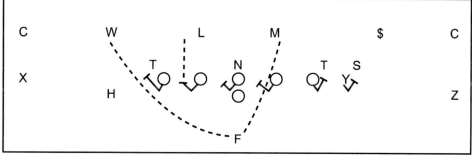

Diagram 3-40: One-Back Zone Protection vs. Okie Front

In one-back formations, we are still only going to free release three receivers into the pattern. The tight end and the slot receiver (in actuality a running back) have simply switched their two-back formation assignments. Both the tight end and the running back remaining in the backfield are assigned check releases. If their designated linebackers drop into coverage, then they run predetermined underneath pass routes and become involved in the pattern.

A definite advantage of the one-back protection scheme is the help that it gives to an offensive lineman when a defender does not blitz. As shown in Diagram 3-33, the right tackle is available to help either the right guard or the tight end if his assigned linebacker drops into coverage. Diagrams 3-34 through 3-36 show this one-back protection scheme against various defensive fronts.

In one-back formations, we can still account for seven potential pass rushers, while releasing a minimum of three receivers into the pattern. Depending on the pass rush, our check-release system gives us the potential to get four or five receivers out into the pattern.

This pass-protection scheme makes it possible for any offensive unit to line up in an unlimited number of one-back formations. It forces the defense to make adjustments in the alignment of its second and third level players, while allowing the offense to be basic and sound in its protection scheme. Diagrams 3-37 and 3-38 illustrate two one-back formations that incorporate the protection scheme.

This protection scheme allows offenses to be versatile in the use of their formations without altering the basic pass-protection scheme. While this scheme may cause the defense to perceive that their opponent has an extremely complex offense that is hard to prepare for, it is still possible for this scheme to be effective despite only running a limited number of basic plays.

We can also use a zone-protection scheme with one-back formations. Ideally, we would slide our zone-protection scheme away from the tight end and have the remaining running back utilize the Scat protection scheme that we have already discussed. This type of protection is shown in Diagram 3-39.

We slide our protection scheme away from the tight end, beginning with the first uncovered offensive lineman. Variations of this protection scheme are shown in Diagrams 3-40 through 3-44. The running back needs to recognize where the uncovered offensive lineman is in our formation, so that he can identify where the Slide will originate.

It is possible to make another adjustment against teams that play Slide Weak, and have a tremendous 7-technique pass rusher aligned over the tight end. In Diagram 3-42, an Out adjustment is made on the tight end side.

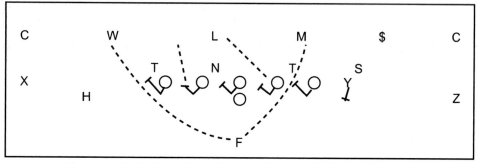

Diagram 3-41: One-Back Protection vs. Slide Weak Front

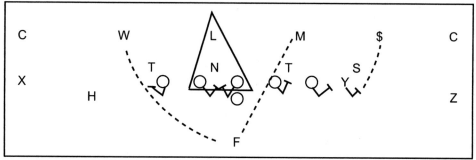

Diagram 3-42: One-Back Protection with Out vs. Slide Weak Front

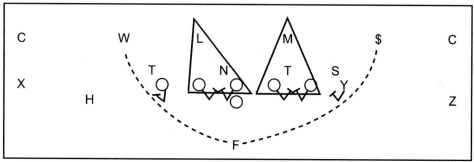

Diagram 3-43: One-Back Protection vs. Strong Eagle Front

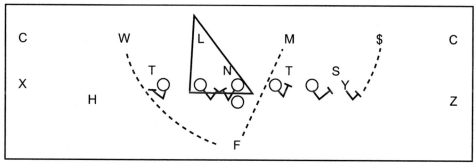

Diagram 3-44: One-Back Protection with Out vs. Strong Eagle Front

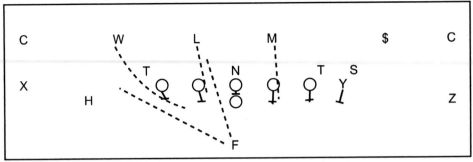

Diagram 3-45: Split End Side Double Read

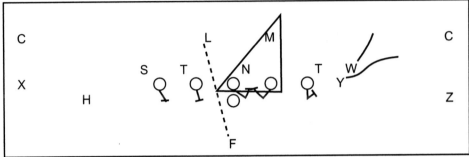

Diagram 3-46: One-Back Protection

It is also possible to make the same adjustment against teams that play Strong Eagle, and have a tremendous 7-technique pass rusher aligned over the tight end. In Diagram 3-44, an Out adjustment is made on the tight end side.

We can employ the Double Read technique into our one-back protection scheme. The uncovered guard and running back can account for four potential pass rushers. In one-back formations, the Double Read is only used on the split-end side of the formation.

The Double-Read scheme is similar to the man pass protection scheme in that any covered offensive lineman must block the defender that is aligned over him on the line of scrimmage. Whenever we get an uncovered guard on the split-end side, we can utilize the Double-Read technique as shown in Diagram 3-45.

The tight end is not involved in the Double Read, but still has a check-release responsibility. If the outside linebacker over him drops into coverage, then the tight end would run a complementary underneath check route. This protection scheme is shown in Diagram 3-46. Three common tight end check releases are shown in Diagrams 3-47 through 3-49.

Some offensive coaches prefer to free release four receivers, whether from one-back or two-back formations. This step gives the offense an opportunity to be much more diverse in the design of patterns by taking advantage of particular defensive secondary coverages, obtaining mismatches, and flooding zones. Obviously, while good in theory

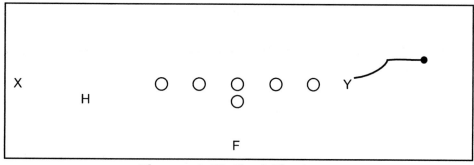

Diagram 3-47: Check Flat Route

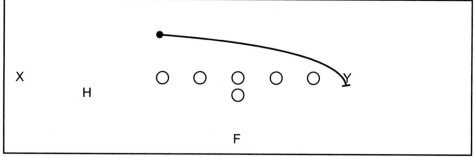

Diagram 3-48: Check Cross Route

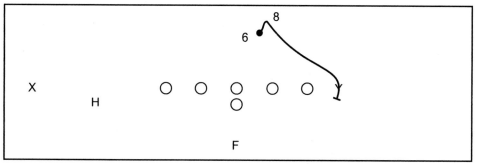

Diagram 3-49: Check Hook Route

and impressive on the chalkboard, these patterns will have no chance to succeed if the quarterback does not have time to deliver the football to the open receiver(s). Five popular formations that allow offenses to get four receivers involved in the pattern are shown in Diagrams 3-50 through 3-54.

A man-protection scheme provides a simple solution to the problem of trying to protect the quarterback with only six offensive players. The man-protection scheme requires the offensive linemen to identify threats along the line of scrimmage, and the running back to account for the remaining potential pass rushers with Scat protection. The Scat scheme makes the remaining running back responsible for two potential second-level pass rushers. The running back will block whichever of the two players be-

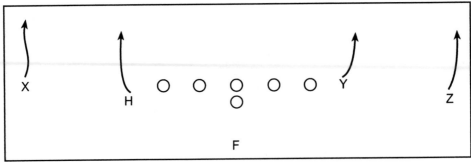

Diagram 3-50: Deuce Right Formation

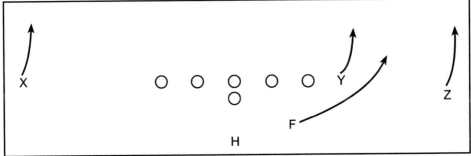

Diagram 3-51: King Right Formation

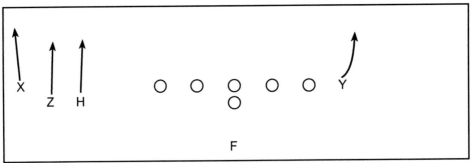

Diagram 3-52: Trips Right Formation

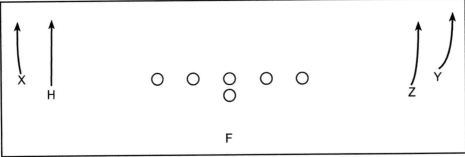

Diagram 3-53: Doubles Right Formation

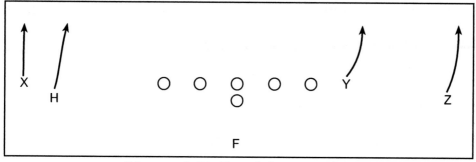

Diagram 3-54: Slot Right Formation

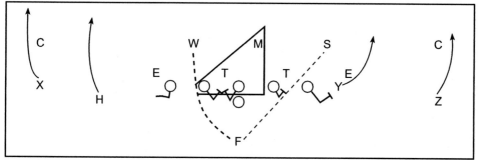

Diagram 3-55: Man Protection with Scat Technique vs. 4-3 Front

comes a pass rusher by blocking the inside pass rusher and allowing the outside pass rusher to come free if both players rush. Diagram 3-55 shows how the Scat technique can be incorporated into man protection with four receivers free released.

The most difficult and time-consuming aspect of incorporating this type of man-protection scheme into an offensive system is making certain that the running back recognizes every defensive front that he will face in the course of a game or season. Diagrams 3-56 through 3-59 show the protection scheme against various fronts.

It is possible to vary the man-protection scheme against defensive units that like to play an Okie front the majority of the time, using Out protection on the tight-end side of the formation, and Scat protection from inside to outside as shown in Diagram 3-57.

When using a protection scheme that allows four receivers to be free released into the pattern, it is critical that the quarterback understand that we can now only account for six pass rushers with our protection scheme. This situation is shown in Diagram 3-60. The running back is coached to always protect the quarterback's blind side first (i.e., the side opposite his throwing arm), and to always block an inside pass rusher before an outside pass rusher.

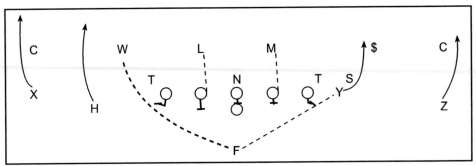

Diagram 3-56: Okie Front

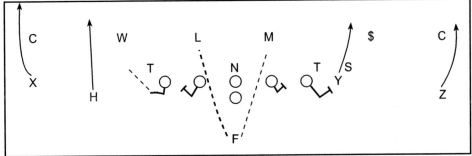

Diagram 3-57: Out Protection vs. Okie

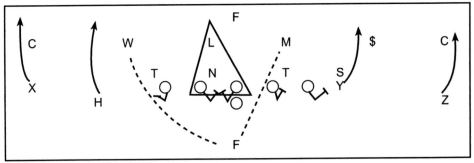

Diagram 3-58: Man Protection vs. Slide Weak Front

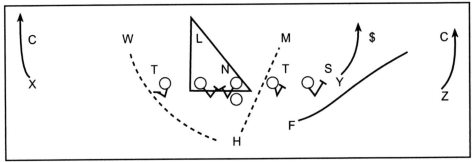

Diagram 3-59: Man Protection vs. Strong Eagle Front

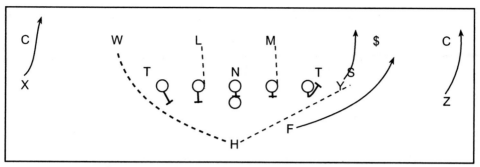

Diagram 3-60: Running Back's Responsibility

Summary

When selecting a five-step drop pass protection scheme (or schemes), an offensive coaching staff must determine which scheme is most readily incorporated into the overall offensive system in which they believe. Questions about how techniques will be taught, how much time will be required to teach those techniques, and whether particular players are capable of utilizing those techniques require answers before a particular scheme can be selected.

PLAY-ACTION
PROTECTION

An effective play-action passing attack is one of the greatest assets that any offensive football team can develop. Nothing increases the overall effectiveness of an offensive unit's passing attack more than the ability to throw the football in down-and-distance situations when the opposing defense is expecting a running play. The ability to run the football and consistently move the chains with an effective ground game provides a tremendous opportunity to utilize a play-action passing attack to throw the football in situations when the defensive is focusing on stopping the run.

Play-action pass protection schemes can and should play an important role in any football team's offensive attack. Offensive coaching staffs committed to running the football can utilize a play-action passing attack to complement and enhance what they do best. Offensive units committed to full-house backfield sets utilizing Wishbone, Power-I, Straight-T, and even Wing-T formations, often rely on a play-action passing attack when they want to throw the ball. Obviously, offensive units that are consistently able to run the football effectively can force opposing defenses into front alignments, secondary coverages, blitzes, and stunts that make throwing the football easier.

Man Protection

By far, the easiest way to protect a play-action pass pattern is to use a man-protection scheme that assigns each offensive lineman to block the same defensive player that he is assigned to block when the play being simulated is normally run. Assume that an offensive unit calls the inside zone running play, illustrated in Diagram 4-1, as a normal part of their run offense.

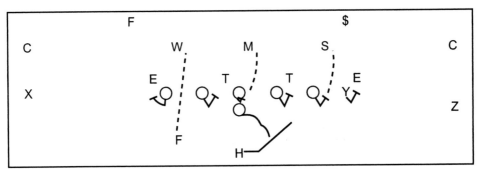

Diagram 4-1: 24 Zone

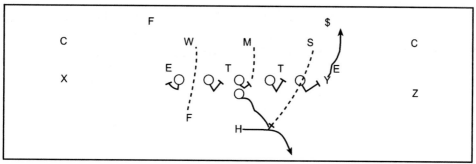

Diagram 4-2: Tackle Bubble

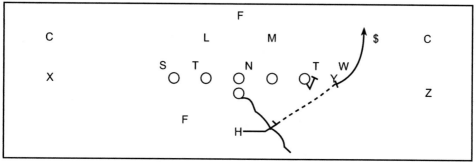

Diagram 4-3: Tackle Covered

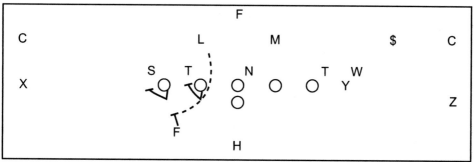

Diagram 4-4: Reduced Defense

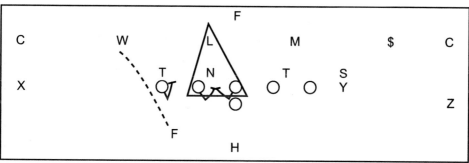

Diagram 4-5: Slide Weak Defense

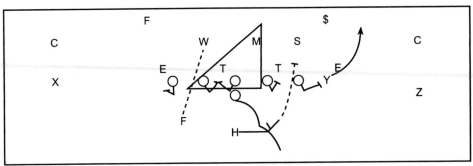

Diagram 4-6: 4-3 Defense

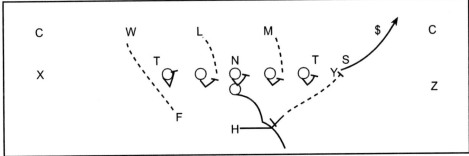

Diagram 4-7: Okie Defense

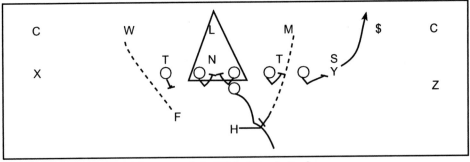

Diagram 4-8: Slide Weak Defense

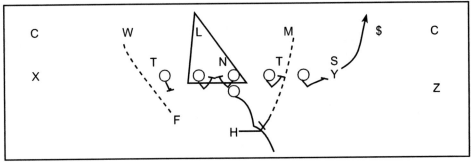

Diagram 4-9: Strong Eagle Defense

The complementary play-action pass protection scheme integrates basic man-protection responsibilities into the scheme that is used to block the base running play. Obviously, the protection scheme needs to account for the tight end who is now going to release into the pattern and run a route. A basic solution makes the offensive tackle adjacent to the tight end responsible for the tight end's blocking assignment whenever there is a tackle bubble, as illustrated in Diagram 4-2.

If the offensive tackle is covered by a defensive player, as illustrated in Diagram 4-3, then the offensive tackle is going to block the player aligned over him and the running back will be responsible for the tight end's normal blocking assignment.

In any two-back formation, the second running back is responsible for the second-level player (linebacker) that cannot be accounted for by the offensive linemen, as illustrated in Diagrams 4-4 and 4-5.

Obviously, the type of running play that is used in the play-action passing attack depends upon how well the offensive unit normally runs the ball. The best way to implement a play-action passing attack is to develop a play-action pass play off of each of the offense's most effective running plays. We want to be able to simulate each of our top running plays in conjunction with a play-action pass. A man-protection scheme is illustrated versus some common defensive fronts in Diagrams 4-6 through 4-9.

The most important aspect of a play-action pass based on a pure man-protection scheme is the ability of the playside offensive linemen to simulate run action with a very aggressive initial block in order to sell the run play to the defensive opponent. On the backside of the simulated play, the offensive tackle needs to utilize a more passive pass-protection technique so that he can protect the quarterback's blindside.

Zone Protection

Some offensive units prefer to utilize a full zone-protection scheme to protect the quarterback when they throw play-action. Each offensive lineman is assigned a gap along the line of scrimmage, and the running backs are assigned to the remaining vulnerable areas in the protection, based upon the defensive front. A basic zone-protection scheme is illustrated in Diagram 4-1

Diagram 4-10 illustrates the slide-gap zone principle. Each offensive lineman is coached to protect his outside gap in the direction of the play being simulated. This is another situation in which we can protect against a maximum of seven pass rushers when we keep both running backs in as part of the protection scheme. We account for the eighth pass rusher by utilizing an audible, automatically adjusting to a quick pass, or making the quarterback aware of where the unaccounted for pass rusher will come from and coaching him to deliver the ball before he arrives. A zone-protection scheme is illustrated versus some common defensive fronts in Diagrams 4-11 through 4-13.

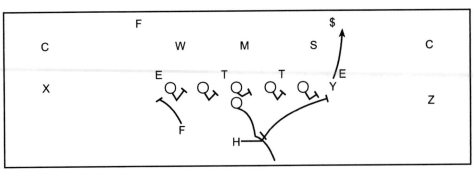

Diagram 4-10: Zone Protection

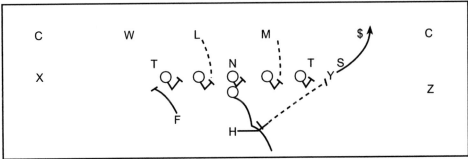

Diagram 4-11: Okie Defense

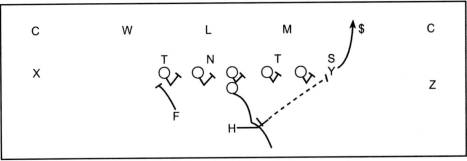

Diagram 4-12: Slide Weak Defense

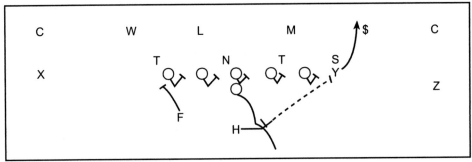

Diagram 4-13: Strong Eagle Defense

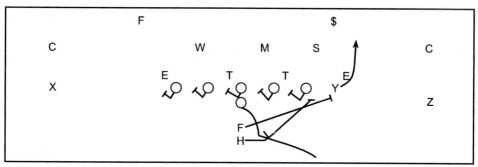

Diagram 4-14: Turn back Protection

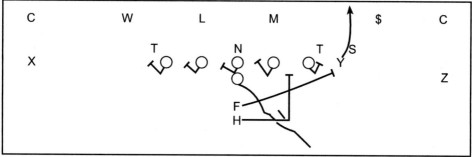

Diagram 4-15: Okie Defense

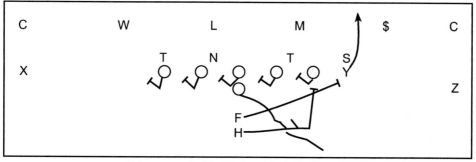

Diagram 4-16: Slide Weak Defense

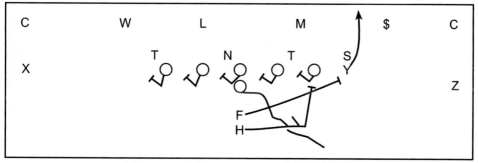

Diagram 4-17: Strong Eagle Defense

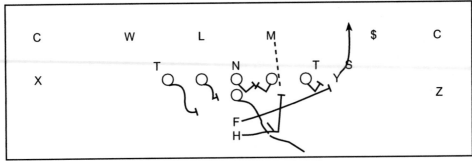

Diagram 4-18: Hinge Protection

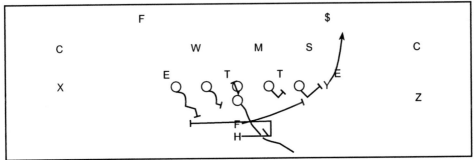

Diagram 4-19: Sprint Draw Pass

Turn-Back Protection

Another type of zone-protection scheme that we can utilize with our play-action passing attack is what we call turn-back protection. This type of zone-protection scheme assigns the offensive linemen to protect a specific gap and allows them to utilize a very aggressive technique to protect that gap. Diagram 4-14 illustrates one type of turn-back protection scheme.

Turn-back protection is most effectively used in conjunction with an I-formation play-action passing attack. The turn-back protection begins with the first uncovered offensive lineman. Starting with this player, every offensive lineman is coached to turn and block his outside gap away from the direction of the play being simulated. Turn-back protection is illustrated versus some common defensive fronts in Diagrams 4-15 through 4-17.

One of the most important coaching points in teaching the turn-back protection scheme is the assignment of the I-formation tailback. If the playside offensive guard is uncovered, then the running back must be prepared to block the second-level player (linebacker). If the playside offensive guard is covered, then the running back must complete an effective play fake and scan the D gap for his protection responsibility.

It is possible to use a combination of man and zone principles to protect our play-action passing attack. We like to use man principles on the frontside (playside) to accu-

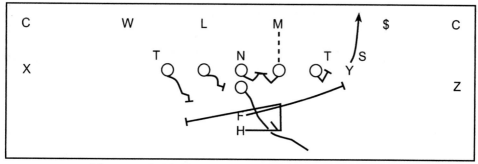

Diagram 3-17: Hot Route Versus Zone Coverage

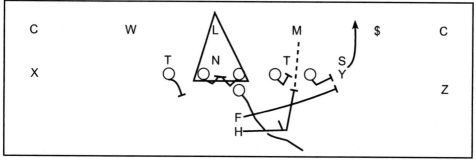

Diagram 3-18: Hot Route Versus Man Coverage

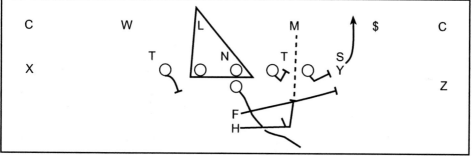

Diagram 3-19: Covered Offensive Tackles

rately simulate our run-blocking schemes and zone principles on the backside to help our offensive linemen. We refer to this backside protection as hinge protection, and prefer to utilize it on the weak side of the formation. This type of zone protection is illustrated in Diagram 4-18.

This protection scheme is best suited to I-formation play-action passing attacks. The tailback is coached to carry out an effective play fake and then protect the backside C gap. This protection scheme is often run in conjunction with some form of sprint-draw play. The sprint-draw pass is illustrated in Diagram 4-19.

This combination of man- and zone-protection schemes is illustrated versus some common defensive fronts in Diagrams 4-20 through 4-22.

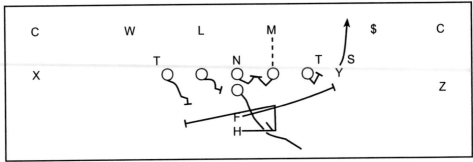

Diagram 4-20: Okie Defense

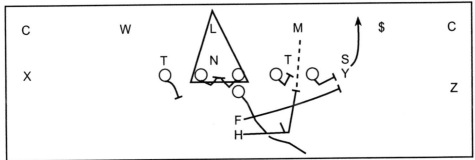

Diagram 4-21: Slide Weak Defense

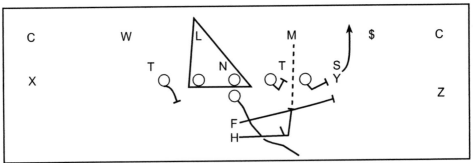

Diagram 4-22: Strong Eagle Defense

Obviously, the offensive coaching staff has some important decisions to make regarding what type of protection scheme(s) to utilize with their particular play-action passing attack. The most important factors are the personnel that they have, the running plays that are consistently most effective for their offensive unit, the formations that they like to use, and their ability to protect against the various defensive fronts that they are seeing from week to week.

We need to consider the adjustments that are necessary in order to develop an effective play-action passing attack from one-back formations. If an offensive unit ever lines up in any form of a one-back formation, then they need to develop some form of play-action pass pattern and protection scheme in order to keep defenses honest against that particular formation.

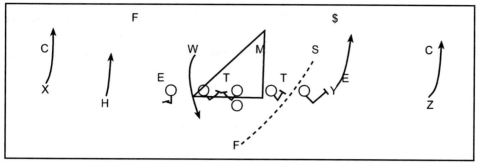

Diagram 4-23: 4-3 Defense

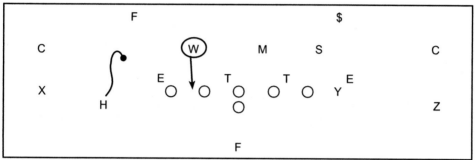

Diagram 4-24: Hot Read and Route

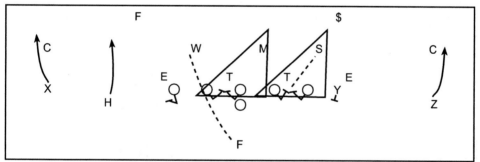

Diagram 4-25: Tight End Kept In

The primary concern of developing a play-action pass-protection scheme for use with one-back formations is the situation in which the defense rushes more people than can be covered by the protection scheme. Obviously, if the defense does bring more people than the offense is assigning to the protection scheme, then the defense has to be able to account for more free-released receivers with fewer defenders dropping into coverage. If the offensive unit is unable to capitalize on this advantage, the defense will undoubtedly continue to bring consistent blitz pressure. Diagram 4-23 illustrates a situation in which the offense has no way to account for a second-level player (the Will linebacker in this case).

If the offensive coaching staff chooses to free release all four receivers at the snap of the ball, then a plan to incorporate a hot or blitz control route into the overall pattern, in

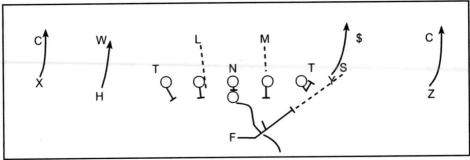

Diagram 4-26: Okie Defense

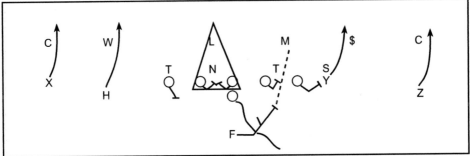

Diagram 4-27: Slide Weak Defense

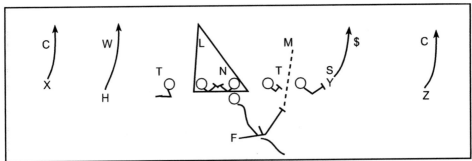

Diagram 4-28: Strong Eagle Defense

order to deal with a pass rushers that cannot be accounted for, is a must. An example of a hot route is illustrated in Diagram 4-24.

A more conservative solution to the problem is to incorporate the tight end (Y) into the protection scheme and free release the split end (X), flanker (Z), and slot receiver (H). This step insures that there are always seven offensive players involved in the protection scheme. This solution is illustrated in Diagram 4-25.

Some offensive coaches are determined to make blitzing and pressure defenses pay a price by releasing four receivers, thus exposing the vulnerability of the resulting secondary coverage. Diagrams 4-26 through 4-28 illustrate three different play-action pass patterns that utilize the protection schemes we have already shown, to deal with unaccounted for pass rushers in the defensive front.

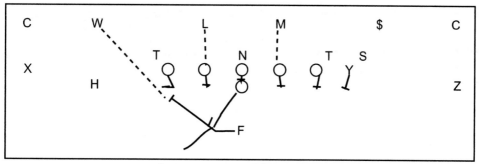

Diagram 4-29: Okie Defense

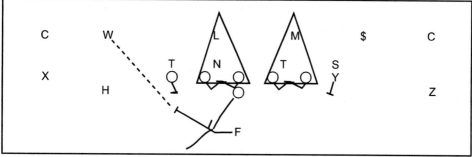

Diagram 4-30: Slide Weak Defense

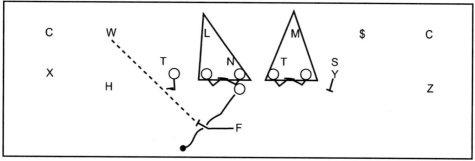

Diagram 4-31: Strong Eagle Defense

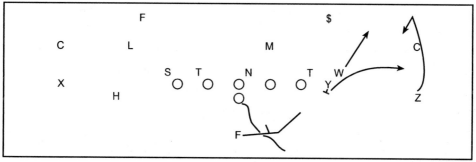

Diagram 4-32: Check Route

It is important that the offensive coaching staff teach the quarterback what to look for during his pre-snap read in order to recognize where potential blitzes are likely to occur. Implementing an effective play-action passing attack requires the quarterback to identify those situations in which he has to rely on some type of hot route adjustment. To avoid using hot routes and to reduce the pressure on the quarterback, as well as the receivers, it may be wise to keep the tight end in as part of the protection scheme. Diagrams 4-29 through 4-31 illustrate three different play-action pass patterns that utilize this type of protection scheme.

In any play-action pass-protection scheme, an important coaching point is to remember that it is always possible to incorporate some form of the check-release concept that we discussed in earlier chapters. By doing so, it is possible to teach any eligible receiver to take advantage of situations in which he is not needed as part of the protection scheme. For example, a tight end (Y) who normally has a pass-protection responsibility in one-back formations is allowed to release into a pass route when the defensive player that is his responsibility drops into pass coverage. Diagram 4-32 illustrates an example of a check route.

The remaining running back should also be coached to take a check release. It is important that he understand which defensive player(s) he is responsible for so that he knows when he can release into a pass route. Every play-action pass pattern should be designed so that all of the check routes complement the routes being run by the receivers who are free released. Diagrams 4-33 and 4-34 illustrate two different types of check routes in which the running back might be involved.

Offenses can also incorporate a one-back zone-protection scheme that assigns the running back to carry out the play fake and protect the playside edge of the formation, while the offensive linemen slide away from the play fake and protect their outside gaps. Diagram 4-35 illustrates the protection scheme when the simulated play is being run to the tight-end side of the formation, and Diagram 4-36 illustrates the same scheme when the simulated play is being run to the split-end side of the formation.

Another one-back protection scheme that combines man and zone principles involves making a fake to the split-end side of the formation, and keeping the tight end in as part of the backside protection scheme. Again, we employ an aggressive man scheme on the front-side (playside) to sell the run play to the defense, and use a hinge technique on the backside. Diagrams 4-37 through 4-40 illustrate this protection scheme.

One last one-back protection scheme to consider is utilized with a different type of one-back formation. We use this formation to free release three receivers from the tight-end side of the formation. In order to remain sound in our protection scheme, we utilize slide-gap zone principles as illustrated in Diagram 4-41 through 4-43.

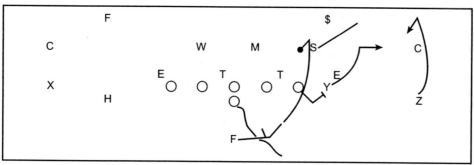

Diagram 4-33: 4-3 Defense

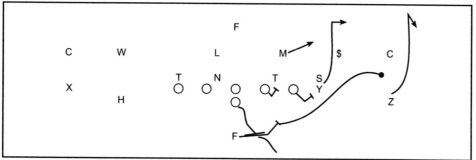

Diagram 4-34: Slide Weak Defense

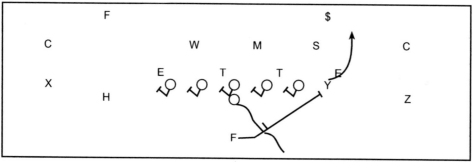

Diagram 4-35: 4-3 Defense

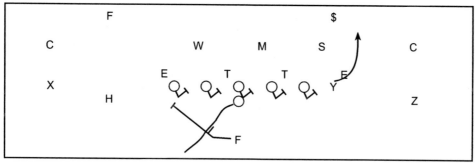

Diagram 4-36: 4-3 Defense

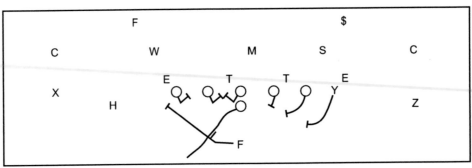

Diagram 4-37: 4-3 Defense

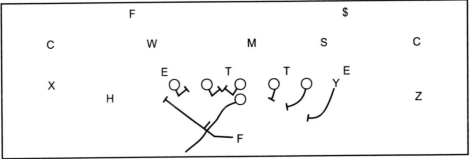

Diagram 4-38: Okie Defense

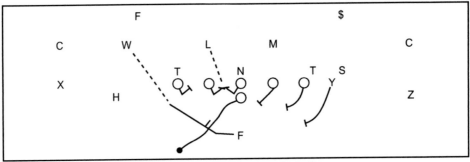

Diagram 4-39: Slide Weak Defense

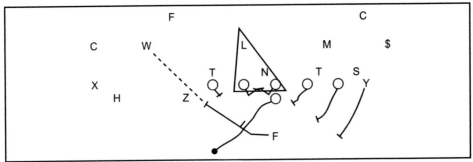

Diagram 4-40: Strong Eagle Defense

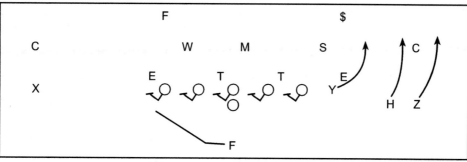

Diagram 4-41: 4-3 Defense

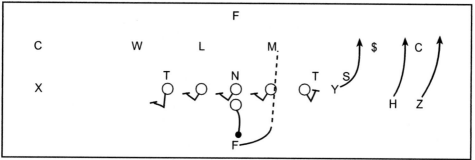

Diagram 4-42: Okie Defense

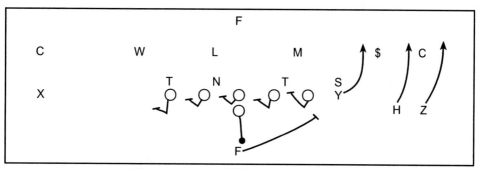

Diagram 4-43: Slide Weak Defense

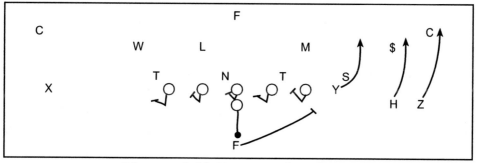

Diagram 4-44: Strong Eagle Defense

Summary

Whether an offensive unit chooses to use one or several play-action pass-protection schemes, we think that it is vitally important that they are able to threaten the defensive opponent with some sort of play-action passing attack. Even teams that are determined to run the football 90 percent of the time (or more), and never drop back to throw the ball, can help themselves by adding a basic and sound play-action attack that is based on the formations and plays that they utilize most often.

CHAPTER 5

BOOT ACTION AND
NAKED PROTECTION

We have already emphasized the importance of an effective play-action passing attack. One way to increase the effectiveness of an offensive unit's play-action passing attack is to incorporate a quarterback run-pass option into the normal play-action attack. The quarterback simulates a basic running play, leaves the pocket, and puts pressure on the perimeter of the defense. While this action gives the offensive unit an obvious advantage, the implementation of an effective protection scheme needs to be a major concern.

We utilize two entirely different protection schemes in conjunction with our basic running schemes in these situations. When we want to use a naked scheme, we simply add the term "naked" to the end of one of our basic running plays. Diagram 5-1 illustrates Queen Right 24 Naked.

The play call tells every member of the offensive unit that we are going to simulate our 24 inside zone play, and utilize play-action with naked protection. The offensive line is coached to know that in naked protection, they are going to block their normal run assignment. They will utilize a much more aggressive pass-protection technique than in normal drop-back pass-protection situations. They must be extremely aggressive in their initial demeanor, remembering that they cannot cross the line of scrimmage and go downfield. Any offensive lineman whose normal run-blocking assignment would be a second-level player (linebacker) is coached to eyeball his assignment. If the assigned player drops into coverage or does not fill aggressively to stop the simulated running play, then the offensive lineman will aggressively seek out any wrong-colored jersey to block.

The fullback has an important assignment in naked protection. In Diagram 5-1, the fullback is coached to blunt the edge of the formation before releasing into the flat. In order for a running back to blunt the edge of the formation, he must be able to identify the contain element within the structure of the defense. The running back wants to maintain outside leverage on the contain element of the defense and strike a blow with his inside arm. This positioning forces the defensive player to come underneath (inside of) the running back when the defensive player makes his charge toward the quarterback. This gives the quarterback a better opportunity to break contain and get outside the perimeter of the defense.

Diagram 5-2 illustrates another protection scheme that can be used in conjunction with a naked play-action scheme. The offensive unit is simulating some type of I formation sweep play, and the quarterback is utilizing naked action to break outside the contain element of the defense.

In this situation, the contain element within the structure of the defense is not going to be blocked at all. The simulation of the sweep play should influence the contain player to close down and chase the tailback from behind, allowing the quarterback to get around and outside of him.

A naked-action play run in conjunction with a long-counter (counter trey) running scheme has become popular in the last decade. Diagram 5-3 illustrates the running play from which the naked-action play is derived. This play is based on what Joe Gibbs and the Washington Redskins were doing in the late 1980's.

The protection scheme is exactly like the simulated long-counter run in that the backside guard and the backside tackle both pull, and the fullback blunts the edge of the formation. The naked action off of the long-counter scheme is illustrated in Diagram 5-4.

The backside guard is coached to clear the center's initial alignment and block the first wrong-colored jersey that appears outside of the B gap. The backside tackle is coached to clear the center's initial alignment and scan inside-to-outside in order to help on any potential pass rushers that appear. The center is coached to block back and actually cross the line of scrimmage, looking back for any pursuit that is attempting to chase the quarterback. Diagram 5-5 illustrates the center's assignment.

The coaching staff should emphasize that the naked-protection scheme is a pure run-blocking scheme intended to help get the quarterback outside of the contain element of the defense. Once the quarterback breaks the containment, he must understand that he has a run-pass option and should take advantage of what the defense is giving up. It is the responsibility of the offensive coaching staff to make certain that the pattern includes at least one route that will allow the quarterback to deliver the ball quickly in the event that he faces quick-blitz pressure by a defender who is not fooled by the run fake.

The naked-action protection scheme can also be utilized from one-back formations without varying the two-back formation protection scheme. Diagram 5-6 illustrates one example.

We also use a variation of our basic naked protection scheme called "naked-stay protection." We prefer to use this protection scheme from one-back formations when we want to guarantee that the quarterback will break contain. When we add a stay call to the play, the halfback knows that he is going to protect the quarterback and not release into the flat. Diagram 5-7 illustrates an example of the naked-stay protection scheme.

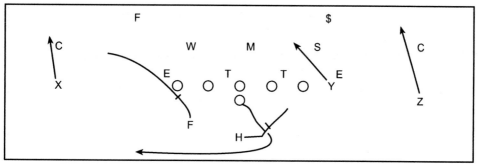

Diagram 5-1: Queen Right 24 Naked

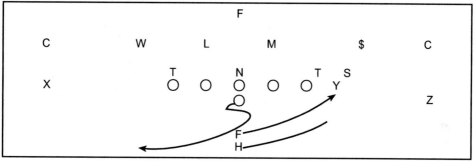

Diagram 5-2: I Sweep Naked

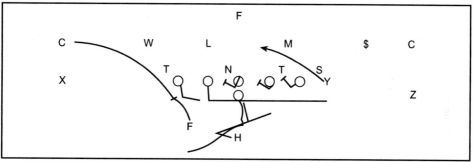

Diagram 5-3: Long Counter Vs Strong Eagle Defense

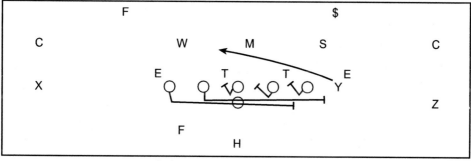

Diagram 5-4: 4-3 Defense

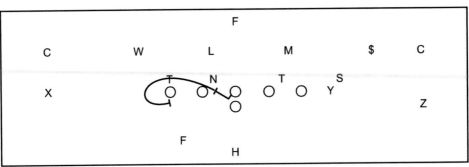

Diagram 5-5: Center's Assignment Vs Slide Weak

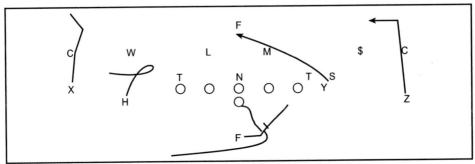

Diagram 5-6: One Back 4-3 Naked Action

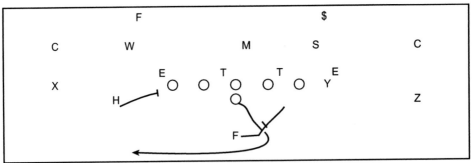

Diagram 5-7: Naked Stay Protection

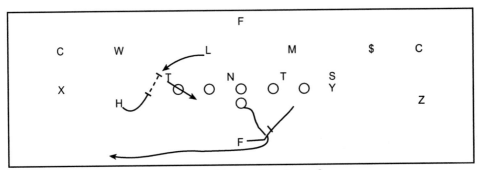

Diagram 5-8: Strong Eagle Defense

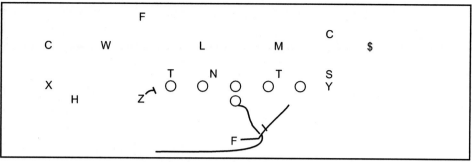

Diagram 5-9: Naked Stay Protection Vs Slide Weak Defense

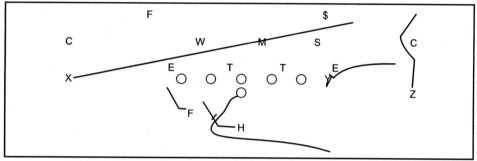

Diagram 5-10: 4-3 Defense

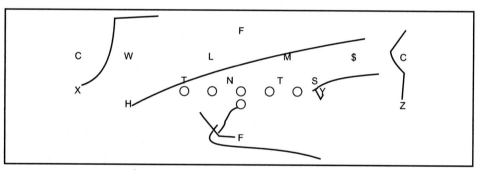

Diagram 5-11: Strong Eagle Defense

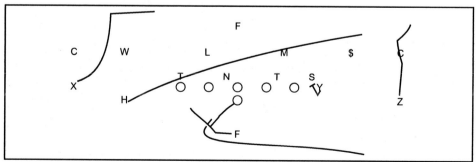

Diagram 5-12: Strong Eagle Defense

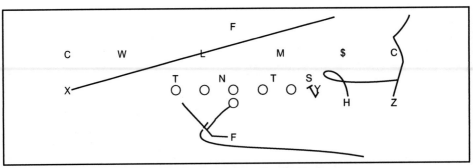

Diagram 5-13: Strong Eagle Defense

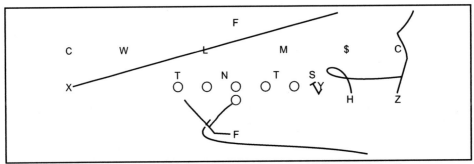

Diagram 5-14: Naked Stay Protection Vs Slide Weak Defense

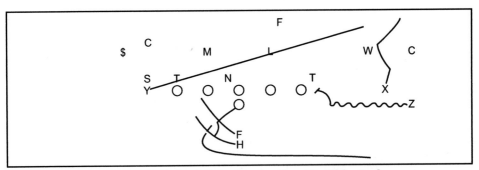

Diagram 5-15: Naked Stay Protection Vs Okie Defense

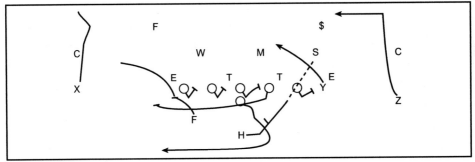

Diagram 5-16: 4-3 Defense

The naked-stay protection scheme provides extra protection for the quarterback on the edge of the defense. This insures that a scraping linebacker will be blocked so that the quarterback can break contain against defenses that are trying to force him to stay in the pocket. Diagram 5-8 illustrates an example.

The naked-stay protection scheme is applicable to a variety of formations. Another example is illustrated in Diagram 5-9.

The naked-action protection scheme also allows the offense to simulate split-end side running plays and break contain to the tight-end side of the defense. Offensive coaching staffs who want to get the quarterback outside of contain on the tight-end side of the formation need to consider two important factors. First, the contain element of the defense is one man wider in his alignment technique and will probably be affected less by the run fake. Second, it is crucial that a second-level crossing route be incorporated in to the pattern. Diagram 5-10 illustrates a potential play utilizing naked action to the tight-end side of a formation. This scheme can also be utilized in conjunction with one-back formations, as illustrated in Diagram 5-11.

While the naked-stay protection scheme can also be utilized on the tight-end side of the formation, we would only utilize this scheme against defenses that utilize an inside-aligned defensive player (7 technique) against our tight end as illustrated in Diagram 5-12.

The naked-stay call dictates that the tight end blocks the 7 technique, helping the quarterback to break contain with naked action to the strongside of the formation, rather than releasing into the route. Diagram 5-13 illustrates an example of this protection scheme.

Two alternative ways of securing the strongside edge of the defense are illustrated in Diagrams 5-14 and 5-15. Both examples utilize the naked-stay scheme. Both of these examples put an outside receiver into short motion. The ball is snapped early so that the receiver has outside leverage on the contain element of the defense and can block him.

We also utilize a boot-action scheme to help get our quarterback outside of the defense's contain element. The boot-action scheme resembles the naked-action protection scheme, but utilizes a pulling guard to block the contain element of the defense. This protection scheme requires that the simulated running play be designed so that the running back can help with the protection scheme. An example of how to blend this action is illustrated in Diagram 5-16. The running back will fill in for the pulling guard and, depending on the defensive front, will provide help to an offensive lineman or have a solo blocking assignment.

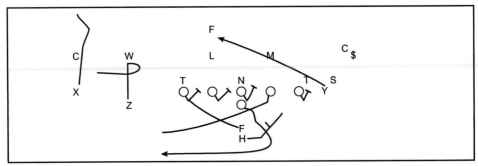

Diagram 5-17: Boot Action Protection Vs Okie Defense

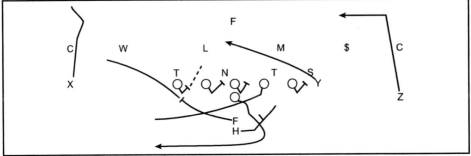

Diagram 5-18: Boot Action Protection Vs. Strong Eagle Defense

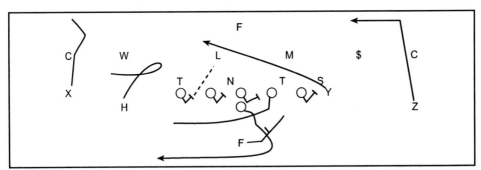

Diagram 5-19: Boot Action Protection Vs Slide Weak Defense

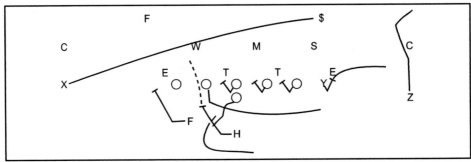

Diagram 5-20: Boot Action Vs. 4-3 Defense

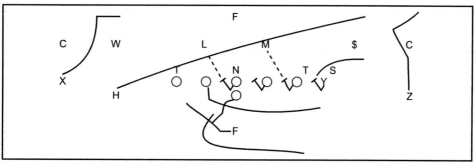

Diagram 5-21: Boot Action Protection Vs Okie Defense

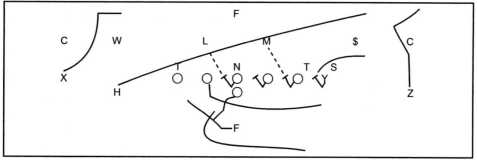

Diagram 5-22: Boot Action Protection Vs. Strong Eagle Defense

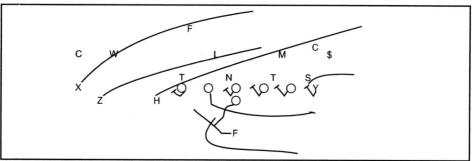

Diagram 5-23: Boot Action Protection Vs Slide Weak Defense

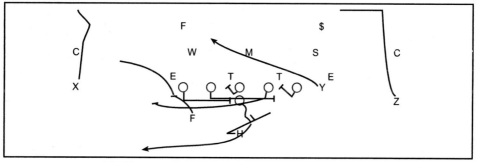

Diagram 5-24: Long Counter Vs 4-3 Defense

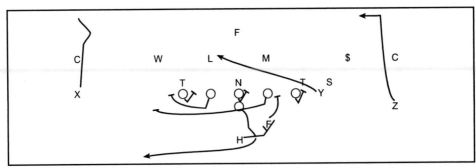

Diagram 5-25: Maximum Boot Protection Vs Okie Defense

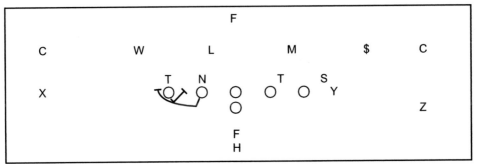

Diagram 5-26: Slide Weak Defense

The pulling guard must be coached to gain depth on his pull to gain leverage on the contain elementof the defense. The pulling guard always wants to get outside leverage, so that the quarterback can get outside and break contain. The pulling guard will only utilize a kick out block if the contain element of the defense gets far up field and is deep in the backfield. Diagrams 5-17 through 5-19 illustrate three different boot-action protection schemes.

In each of these examples, a running play is being simulated in one direction, and the quarterback is booting out in the opposite direction. It is also possible to simulate a running play to the split-end side of the formation and have the quarterback attempt to break contain on the tight-end side of the formation. Diagram 5-20 illustrates an example of such a play.

It is also possible to utilize the boot-protection scheme from any of several one-back formations. Three possibilities are illustrated in Diagrams 5-21 through 5-23.

We can also utilize the boot-action play in conjunction with the long-counter running scheme that we showed earlier. Diagram 5-24 illustrates the long-counter boot play. The danger of the boot scheme is the potential for the two offensive guards to collide as they pull in opposite directions. The boot guard must be coached to get extreme depth quickly upon his release from the line of scrimmage.

In some situations, it may be desirable to pull both guards in order to provide maximum protection on the edge of the formation. This is especially the case in offensive systems that rely upon athletic quarterbacks who are a tremendous threat once they get to the edge of the defense and break contain. This maximum-boot scheme is illustrated in Diagram 5-25.

The playside pulling guard must be coached to take a flat, pull step in order to get outside leverage on the first wrong-colored jersey that appears along the line of scrimmage. The second guard takes a normal boot path looking to block any defender that comes up out of coverage in order to contain the quarterback, including a linebacker scraping across on the second level. At any time, the quarterback can utilize his run option and make a go call to inform offensive linemen that they can now go up field.

In situations where both the split-side guard and split-side tackle are covered, an adjustment has to be made. The offensive tackle will block down, and the offensive guard will step around to block the contain element of the defense. This adjustment is illustrated in Diagram 5-26.

The naked and boot packages force the defense to defend the entire field. An athletic quarterback, who is a threat to break contain and be effective in the open field, can eliminate certain blitzes and line movements that defensive teams like to use to pressure quarterbacks who like to remain in the pocket. Obviously the offensive coaching staff needs to be able to select its favorite running plays and fit the boot and naked-action protection schemes into them. The most effective naked and boot protection schemes will undoubtedly be run from formations in which the offense can simulate their most effective bread-and-butter running plays.

CHAPTER 6

SPRINT-OUT
PROTECTION

When the quarterback utilizes sprint-out action in conjunction with a pass-protection scheme, the defense is forced to play sound perimeter run defense while defending the entire field against a well designed passing attack. Sprint-out pass protection schemes are most effective when used with offensive styles of attack that emphasize the running threat of an athletic quarterback. A quarterback who is also a tremendous open-field running threat has the potential to be an excellent sprint-out passer. If the defensive coaching staff has to be concerned with the threat of the quarterback breaking contain and having a run or pass option on every play, then they will begin to stray from the fronts that they like to play in normal down and distance situations.

Strongside Sprint-Out Series Protection Schemes

As always, there are several possible protection schemes that can be used to protect the quarterback in a sprint-out attack. We will start with schemes used to protect the quarterback when he attacks the tight-end side of the formation. This is simply referred to as our strongside sprint-out series. Diagram 6-1 illustrates a basic strongside sprint-out series.

The first type of pass protection scheme that can be used to protect the strongside sprint-out series is a pure zone-protection scheme that involves both running backs in the protection scheme. In this scheme, every offensive player who is involved in the protection has an assigned zone for which he is responsible. When we are going to sprint-out to the right, the strongside (right) offensive tackle is responsible for the right C gap. This zone responsibility is illustrated in Diagram 6-2.

When initially aligned, the right tackle is coached to know that he is responsible for the area between his nose and the nose of the tight end. The tackle employs a technique that dictates he take a lead step with his right foot and keep his shoulders square to the line of scrimmage. When the tackle makes contact with any wrong-colored jersey in his zone, he is coached to slightly work his hips toward the sideline to which the quarterback is sprinting out. We tell the tackle that he must get leverage on the defensive player who is responsible for the C gap.

When we are going to sprint-out to the right, the strongside (right) offensive guard is responsible for the right B gap. This zone responsibility is illustrated in Diagram 6-3.

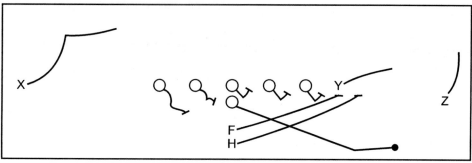

Diagram 6-1: Strongside Sprint-Out Series

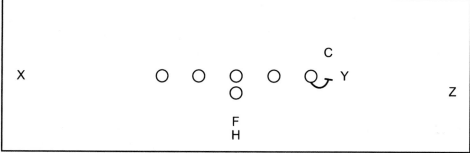

Diagram 6-2: Right Tackle's Assignment

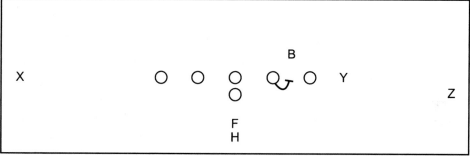

Diagram 6-3: Right Guard's Assignment

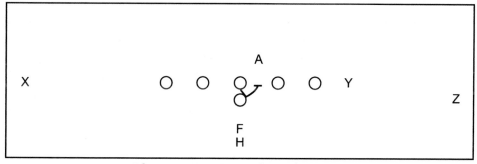

Diagram 6-4: Center's Assignment

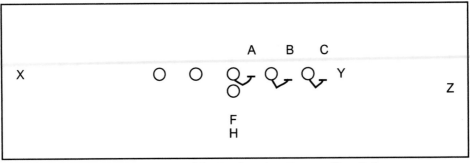

Diagram 6-5: Strongside Sprint-Out Protection Scheme

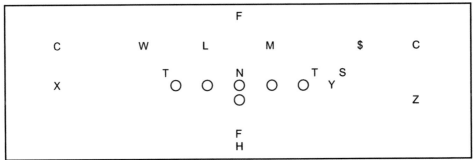

Diagram 6-6: Okie Defense

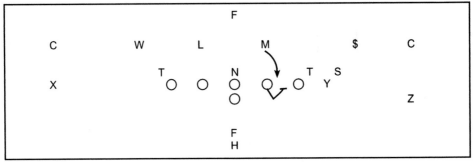

Diagram 6-7: Okie Defense – Slant Weak

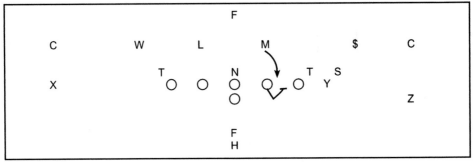

Diagram 6-8: Okie Defense – Linebacker Blitz

When initially aligned, the right guard is coached to know that he is responsible for the area between his nose and the nose of the right tackle. The guard also employs a technique that dictates he take a lead step with his right foot and keep his shoulders square to the line of scrimmage. When the guard makes contact with any wrong-colored jersey in his zone, he is coached to slightly work his hips toward the sideline to which the quarterback is sprinting out. We tell the guard that he must get leverage on the defensive player who is responsible for the B gap.

When the quarterback sprints out to the right, the center takes a lead step with his right foot and keeps his shoulders square to the line of scrimmage. When the center makes contact with any wrong-colored jersey in his zone, he is coached to slightly work his hips toward the sideline to which the quarterback is sprinting out. We tell the center that he must get leverage on the defensive player who is responsible for the A gap. Diagram 6-4 illustrates the center's responsibility.

When we utilize the strongside sprint-out series, the protection scheme looks like Diagram 6-5.

An important coaching point needs to be made concerning what the offensive lineman is coached to do when he is uncovered and there is no threat to his assigned gap. Such an alignment is illustrated in Diagram 6-6.

Whenever a defensive front includes a *bubble* alignment over an offensive lineman, the uncovered offensive lineman must always make sure that one of the adjacent defensive linemen does not slant into his assigned gap. After checking for a possible slant along the line of scrimmage, the eyes of the uncovered offensive lineman must move to the second level looking for a linebacker with the potential to blitz. Diagrams 6-7 and 6-8 illustrate two such scenarios.

When running our strongside sprint-out series, we can use the running backs to guarantee that the quarterback is given an opportunity to break contain. One effective adjustment to the basic zone protection scheme assigns both running backs to protect the D gap. Diagram 6-9 illustrates this scheme.

The tandem of backs work together to secure the D gap, blocking the contain element of the defensive structure. The technique used would dictate that the fullback block the inside half of the defender, while the halfback gains leverage on the outside half of the defender. This technique is illustrated in Diagram 6-10.

Assigning both running backs to the protection scheme allows the offense to pick up any potential extra blitzes on the strongside of the formation. This is illustrated in Diagram 6-11.

The adjustment to pick up such a blitz is easy to teach. The fullback is coached to always secure the D gap, while the halfback is coached to pick up any blitzing defender

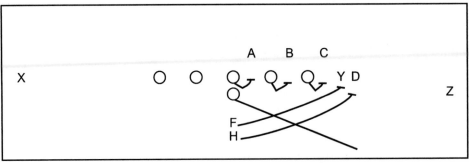

Diagram 6-9: Running Back's Assignment

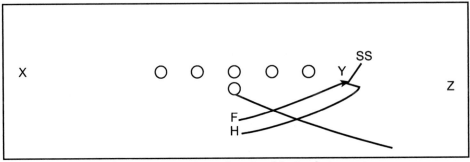

Diagram 6-10: Running Back's Assignment

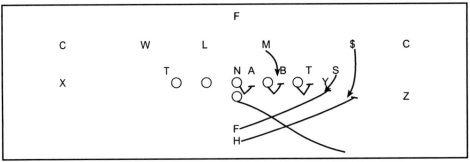

Diagram 6-11: Strongside Safety Blitz

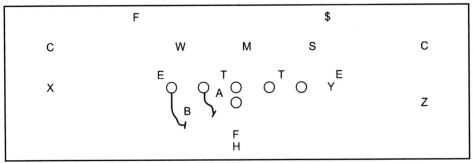

Diagram 6-12: Hinge Technique

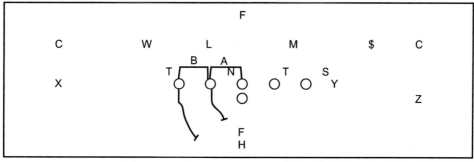

Diagram 6-13: Strong Eagle Defense

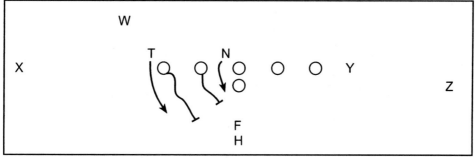

Diagram 6-14: Backside Pass Rush

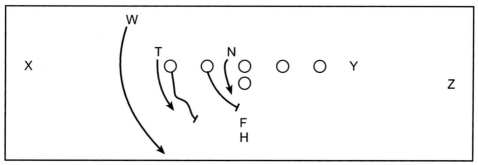

Diagram 6-15: Backside Pass Rush

coming from farther outside. This protection scheme gives the offense maximum protection to the frontside (or strongside) of the play and helps insure that the quarterback will be able to break contain and get outside of the force element in the structure of the defense.

We also utilize a true zone-protection scheme on the backside of the formation. The backside guard and tackle use a blocking technique that we describe as a hinge scheme. They try to gain depth while obtaining an inside leverage position that forces the defender to go outside of their release from the line of scrimmage. The hinge technique is illustrated in Diagram 6-12.

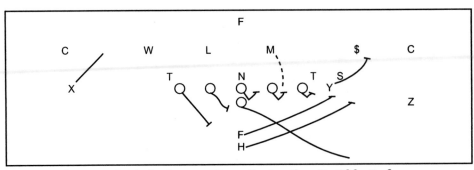

Diagram 6-16: Sprint-out Pass Protection Vs Okie Defense

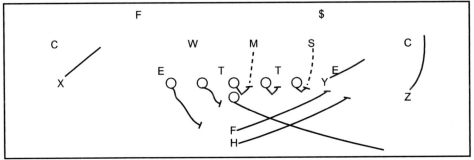

Diagram 6-17: Sprint-out Pass Protection Vs. 4-3 Defense

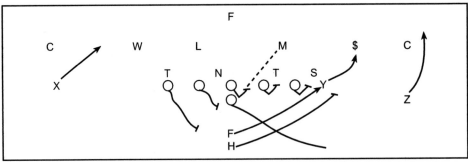

Diagram 6-18: Sprint-out Pass Protection Vs. Strong Eagle Defense

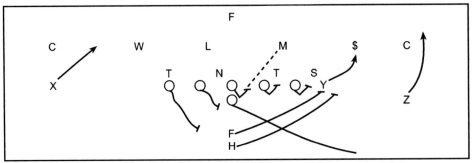

Diagram 6-19: Sprint-out Protection Vs Slide Weak Defense

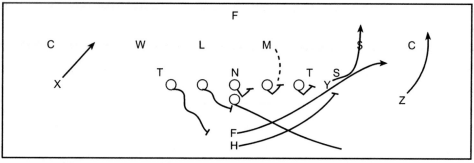

Diagram 6-20: Sprint-out Pass Protection Vs Okie Defense

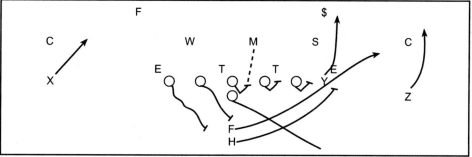

Diagram 6-21: Sprint-out Pass Protection Vs. 4-3 Defense

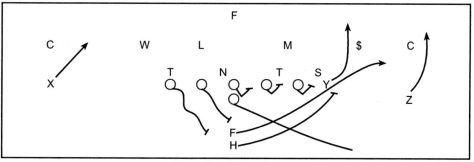

Diagram 6-22: Sprint-out Pass Protection Vs. Strong Eagle Defense

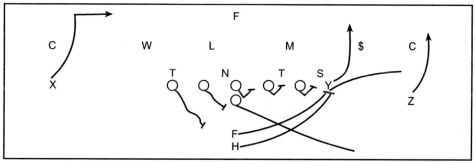

Diagram 6-23: Sprint-out Pass Protection Vs Slide Weak Defense

The backside offensive linemen utilize the same principle as the frontside offensive linemen. The left guard is responsible for the zone extending from his nose to the nose of the center. The zones on the backside are deeper and farther inside than the zones on the frontside. Diagram 6-13 illustrates the details of each zone.

We must account for a defensive player who is shaded on the outside of the center, or the inside of the guard on the side of the formation to which the quarterback is sprinting out. To deal with this problem, the backside guard must be coached to kick back for depth and width to get an inside-leverage position. A major coaching point to remember is that we will never block any backside pass rusher who is coming outside of the B gap. Our quarterback is taught to stay on the move when we utilize this scheme. He knows that he cannot stop and set up because we will not be protecting any potential pass rusher coming through the C Gap. Diagrams 6-14 and 6-15 illustrate the problem.

Diagrams 6-16 through 6-19 illustrate typical strongside sprint-out series protection schemes versus a variety of defensive fronts.

The protection scheme allows the offense to be sound against any defensive front that the opposition wants to play. In order to gain an advantage by adjusting the pass pattern itself, offenses can allow the fullback to seep out into a predetermined route, using him to control the drop of the defender responsible for the flat. This is illustrated in Diagrams 6-20 to 6-23. A major coaching point to remember, when utilizing this scheme, is that the fullback's assignment is to help control blitzes from the strongside of the formation. The offense still needs to be able to account for blitzes from the frontside. Diagram 6-24 illustrates a way for the offense to deal with the extra rusher from the frontside.

Offenses are not limited to using the I formation if they wish to incorporate the zone sprint-out pass-protection scheme. Diagrams 6-25 and 6-26 illustrate two formations that can be used with the strongside sprint-out series.

It is also possible to use a turn-back protection scheme in conjunction with the sprint-out series passing attack. This is an excellent alternative to utilizing the strongside sprint-out zone-protection scheme that has been discussed so far. Diagram 6-27 illustrates the basic scheme.

The turn-back protection scheme gives the offensive line a leverage advantage and allows them to block back or down on the defensive linemen or the second-level players. The responsibilities of the offensive linemen are taught as illustrated in Diagram 6-28.

When sprinting out to the right, the offensive right tackle is coached to lose a little ground with his inside (left) foot in order to secure his inside (left) gap. If the right tackle does not have a defensive lineman aligned in his inside gap or over him, then he would step down and look for a second-level player to blitz or stunt into his assigned gap. This situation is illustrated in Diagram 6-29.

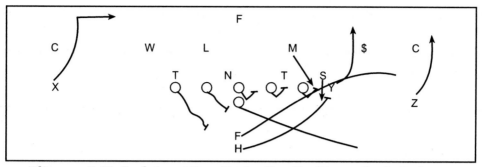

Diagram 6-24: Sprint-out Pass Protection Vs. Strong Eagle Defense

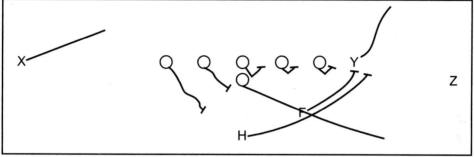

Diagram 6-25: King Right Formation

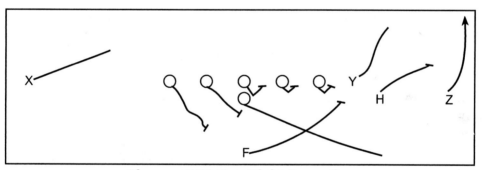

Diagram 6-26: Trey Right Formation

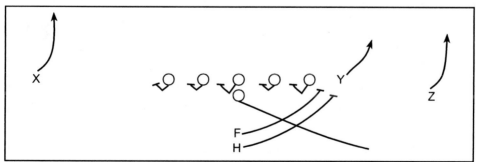

Diagram 6-27: Turn-back Protection Scheme

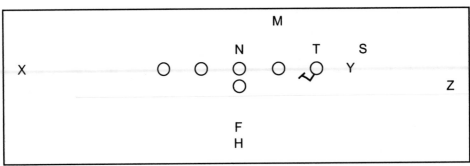

Diagram 6-28: Turn-back Protection Scheme

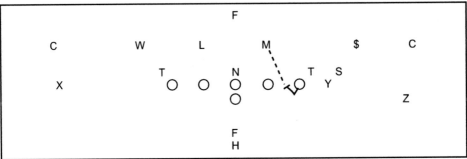

Diagram 6-29: Okie Defense

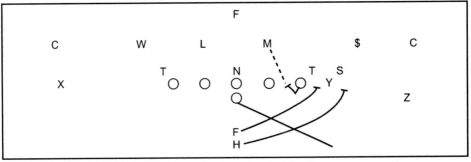

Diagram 6-30: Running Backs' Assignments

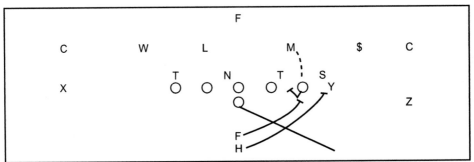

Diagram 6-31: Running Backs' Assignments

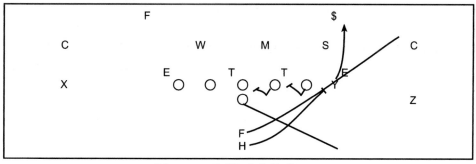

Diagram 6-32: 4-3 Defense

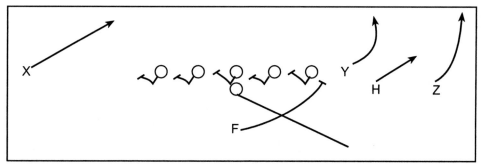

Diagram 6-33: Trey Right Formation

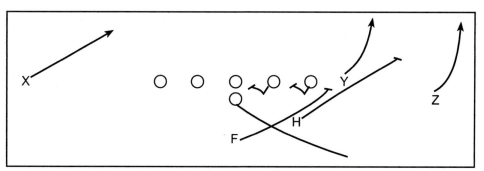

Diagram 6-34: King Right Formation

Each offensive lineman would employ the same technique as the offensive right tackle. The running backs also become involved in this protection scheme. The fullback is responsible for protecting the C gap, and the halfback is responsible for the D gap or any outside blitz. If no defender is assigned to the D gap, then the halfback can help the fullback with the C gap. Diagrams 6-30 and 6-31 illustrate these assignments.

This protection scheme requires the running backs to block bigger and stronger defensive players than in the sprint-out zone protection scheme discussed earlier. It is imperative that the running backs be coached to use the correct technique in securing the strongside C and D gaps.

When using the turn-back sprint-out protection, it is still possible to make a route adjustment, allowing the fullback to become involved in the pattern, and assigning the halfback to the C gap. This adjustment is illustrated in Diagram 6-32.

A hot scheme needs to be employed in the event that we get a C gap blitz and a D gap blitz from the defense. The fullback should be ready to receive the ball quickly in the flat. Diagrams 6-33 and 6-34 illustrate some of the formations that can be utilized with the turn-back protection scheme.

Both the pure zone scheme and the turn-back scheme are very effective when the quarterback sprints out to the strongside of the formation.

Weakside Sprint-Out Series Protection Schemes

Certain aspects of the sprint-out attack must be altered when the quarterback attacks the split-end side of the formation. In certain situations, the weakside sprint-out series gives the offense the advantage of being able to attack the perimeter of the defense faster, due to the lack of a tight end. Most defenses use fewer alignments to the split-end side of the formation, and the secondary coverages are usually less complex on the weakside as well.

One possible protection scheme utilizes full zone protection on the frontside and hinge protection on the backside. The frontside (left) offensive tackle is responsible for the zone extending from his nose to the nose of the *ghost* tight end which would constitute the C Gap. This assignment is illustrated in Diagram 6-35.

The front side (left) offensive guard is responsible for the zone extending from his nose to the nose of the left offensive tackle, which would constitute the B gap. The guard takes a lead step with his left foot and keeps his shoulders square to the line of scrimmage, reading any down player along the line of scrimmage. The guard is responsible for the B gap. This assignment is illustrated in Diagram 6-36.

The center is responsible for the zone extending from his nose to the nose of the left offensive guard, which would constitute the play side A gap. The center's assignment is illustrated in Diagram 6-37.

In a full zone protection scheme, the running backs are made responsible for the playside D gap. The fullback is coached to block the inside half of any defensive player that appears in the D gap, and the halfback is coached to block the outside half while gaining leverage on that defender. If there are two defensive players assigned to the D gap, then the fullback blocks the inside pass rusher, and the halfback blocks the outside pass rusher. A major advantage of sprinting out to the split-end side of the formation is that there will not be much variation in how the defense chooses to contain the quarterback on his sprint-out path. Diagram 6-38 illustrates the running backs' protection responsibility.

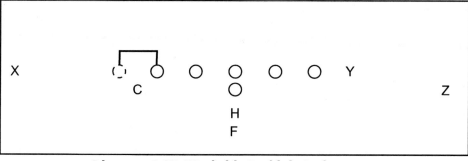

Diagram 6-35: Weakside Tackle's Assignment

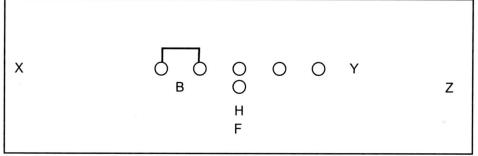

Diagram 6-36: Weakside Guard's Assignment

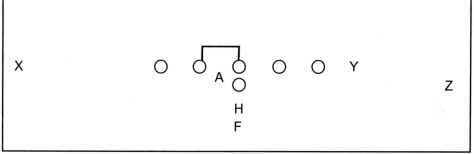

Diagram 6-37: Center's Assignment

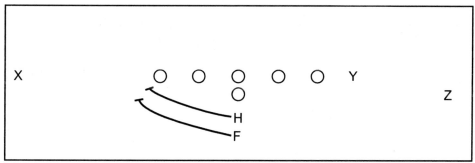

Diagram 6-38: Running Backs' Assignment

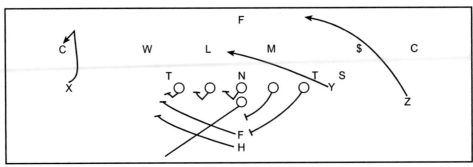

Diagram 6-39: Okie Defense

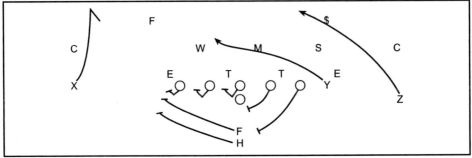

Diagram 6-40: 4-3 Defense

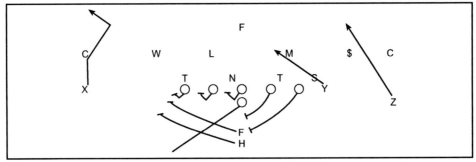

Diagram 6-41: Strong Eagle Defense

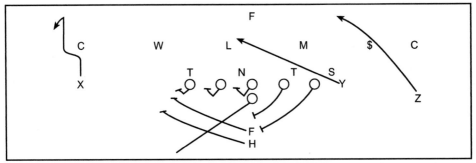

Diagram 6-42: Slide Weak Defense

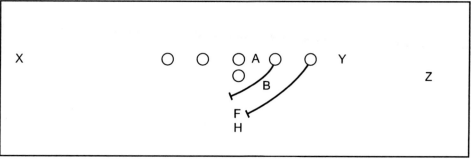

Diagram 6-43: Hinge Protection

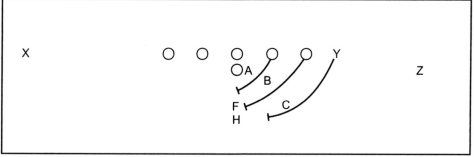

Diagram 6-44: Tight End Adjustment

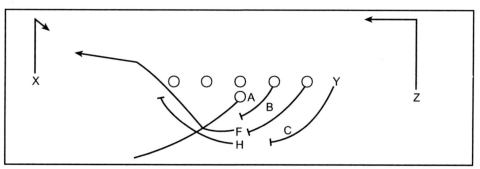

Diagram 6-45: Tight End Adjustment

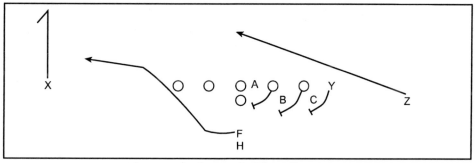

Diagram 6-46: Backside Adjustment

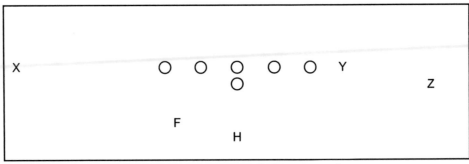

Diagram 6-47: Queen Right Formation

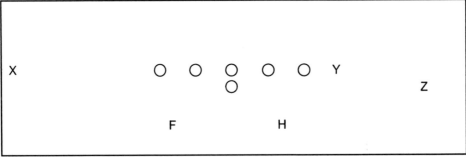

Diagram 6-48: Pro Split Right Formation

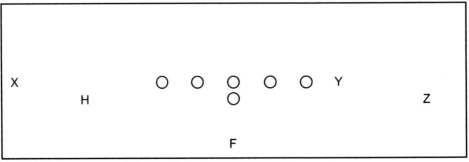

Diagram 6-49: Deuce Right Formation

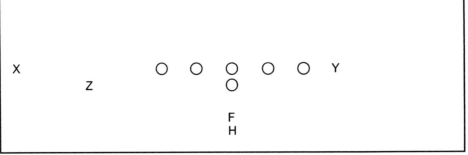

Diagram 6-50: I Twins Right Formation

A disadvantage of the weakside sprint-out series is that offenses only have one frontside receiver available to run a pass route. Several formation adjustments, such as twins, provide a combination of routes to use on the weakside of the formation. Diagrams 6-39 through 6-42 illustrate some potential one-receiver pass routes and appropriate protection schemes versus various defensive fronts.

Hinge protection is used on the backside of our weakside, sprint-out protection scheme. The backside offensive guard and tackle must set up inside and deep in order to protect the backside A and B gaps. Diagram 6-43 illustrates hinge protection.

This protection scheme leaves the C gap unprotected. The quarterback must be coached to stay on the move when he sprints out. An adjustment can be made to include the tight end in the hinge protection scheme on the backside, assigning him to protect the C gap. Diagram 6-44 illustrates this adjustment.

Obviously, this protection scheme provides increased protection on the backside, especially against defenses that like to bring blitz pressure from the strongside of the formation. At the same time, it is important to remember that there is a distinct disadvantage in eliminating one of the backside receivers from the pattern. To offset this, we can vary the basic scheme and release the fullback into the pattern from any two-back formation. This will leave only the halfback to protect versus any type of D gap blitz scheme. While this allows us to attack the secondary coverage with a greater combination of complementary pass routes, we are left with one running back in the protection scheme. Diagram 6-45 illustrates a potential sprint-out pattern based on this protection scheme.

These two adjustments can be combined into another protection scheme. We can keep the tight end in on the backside of the formation to protect the C gap and allow the fullback to release into the pattern on the front (play) side. This adjustment is illustrated in Diagram 6-46.

It is important that offensive coaching staffs make use of their team's ability to align in multiple formations in order to make the weakside sprint-out series more effective. Diagrams 6-47 through 6-49 illustrate three examples of potential formation adjustments.

As mentioned earlier in this chapter, a twins formation can be utilized to maximize protection, while offering the availability of several combinations of pass routes to the twins side of the formation. Diagram 6-50 illustrates a formation offering these advantages.

Twins formations offer offenses a variety of pass-route schemes that are difficult for the secondary to defend, while keeping both running backs in to protect the frontside D gap. Hinge protection on the backside is used to secure the A, B, and C gaps. Diagrams 6-51 through 6-54 illustrate the twins scheme against four typical defenses.

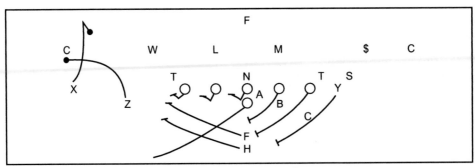

Diagram 6-51: Okie Defense

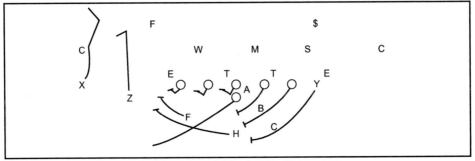

Diagram 6-52: 4-3 Defense

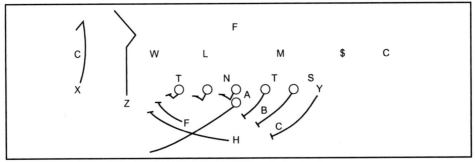

Diagram 6-53: Strong Eagle Defense

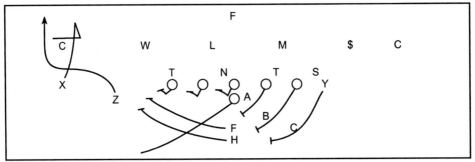

Diagram 6-54: Slide Weak Defense

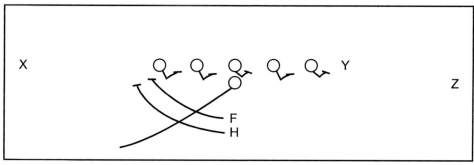

Diagram 6-55: Turn-back Protection

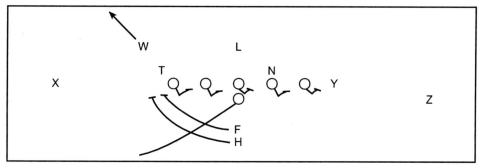

Diagram 6-56: Linebacker Drop

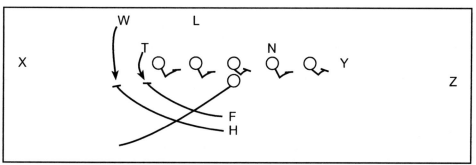

Diagram 6-57: Linebacker Blitz

We can also utilize a turn-back protection scheme with the weakside, sprint-out series to attack the split-end side of the formation. The turn-back scheme is actually pure zone protection. The offensive tackle, on the split-end side of the formation, blocks down on the B gap, and every other offensive lineman turns back and secures the corresponding gap. The turn-back scheme is illustrated in diagram 6-55.

The running backs have protection responsibilities in the turn-back scheme. The fullback is responsible for protecting the C gap, and the halfback is responsible for protecting the D gap or any outside blitz. If no pass rusher appears in the D gap, then the halfback can help the fullback secure the C gap. Diagrams 6-56 and 6-57 illustrate the running backs' assignments.

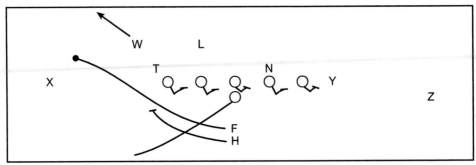

Diagram 6-58: Linebacker Drop

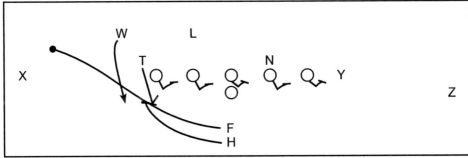

Diagram 6-59: Linebacker Blitz

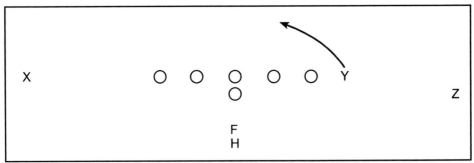

Diagram 6-60: Tight End Release

We can alter the turn-back scheme by releasing the fullback into the pattern and assigning the halfback to protect the C gap. This protection scheme must be used with a built-in fullback hot route that would account for a D gap blitz. With this scheme, it is impossible to account for a D gap pass rusher when the fullback is free released into the pattern. Diagrams 6-58 and 6-59 illustrate this situation.

An important advantage of the turn-back protection scheme is the potential to free release the tight end into the pattern on a route that crosses the formation. We can free release the tight end because the A, B, and C gaps are secured on the backside of the play. This scheme is illustrated in diagram 6-60.

These sprint-out schemes give the offense a way to attack the perimeter of the defense with a run or pass option. Effective protection schemes make it possible to put extreme stress on the edges of the pass defense. They can be an effective and viable part of virtually any style of offensive attack.

CHAPTER 7

DASH
PROTECTION

Another type of pass-protection scheme available to offensive coaching staffs is what is called dash protection. The Denver Broncos popularized dash-protection schemes in the 1980's. In dash-protection schemes, the quarterback appears to set up in the pocket. He then moves to his left or to his right outside of the pocket, setting up near one of the hash marks. The quarterback's technique is sometimes referred to as *dash to the hash*. Diagram 7-1 illustrates a basic dash-protection scheme.

The most important aspect of the dash-protection scheme is getting the quarterback outside of the contain element of the defense. Dash is most effective when used primarily as a weakside scheme, because it is more difficult to *pin* the contain element of the defense on the strongside of the formation.

The offensive tackle on the split-end side of the formation has the most important responsibility in the dash-protection scheme. He must invite the contain element of the defense inside in order to gain outside leverage. This is crucial to the dash-protection scheme, because it allows the quarterback to get outside of the contain element of the defense. This is illustrated in diagram 7-2.

The coaching staff must give the tackle different sets in order to give the defender the impression that he can get to the inside rush lane on the dash scheme.

The offensive guard, on the split-end side of the formation, has both an uncovered rule and a covered rule. If the guard is uncovered, he will set for depth and then pull to the side that the dash is going. The guard maintains an angle to protect the quarterback from the first wrong-colored jersey that appears. The guard must first look outside, and then look inside for a scraping inside linebacker. This is illustrated in Diagrams 7-3 and 7-4.

If the guard is covered, then he sets up for pass protection and blocks the down lineman aligned over him. Against fronts that cover the offensive guard on the split-end side of the formation, the offensive guard will never get out to pull for dash protection. Diagrams 7-5 and 7-6 illustrate two such fronts.

In dash protection, the center also has both a covered rule and an uncovered rule. If a head-up or a shaded defensive player aligns over the center, then the center is responsible to block that down lineman. Diagrams 7-7 through 7-9 illustrate the three possible alignments.

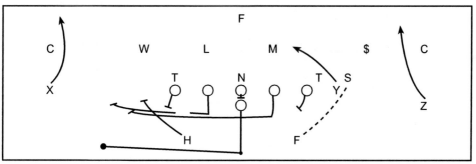

Diagram 7-1: Dash Protection Scheme

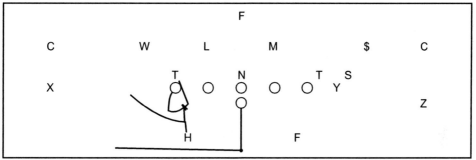

Diagram 7-2: Split End Side Tackle

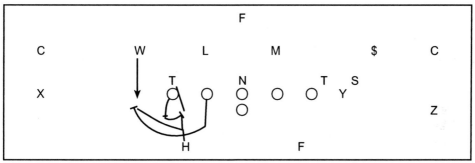

Diagram 7-3: Blitzing Outside Linebacker

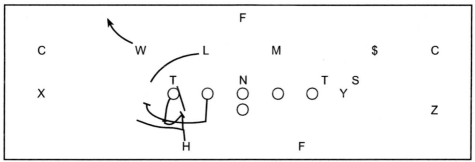

Diagram 7-4: Scraping Inside Linebacker

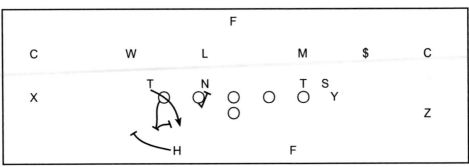

Diagram 7-5: 2i Technique

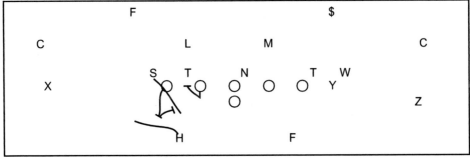

Diagram 7-6: 3 Technique

If the center is uncovered, then he blocks back for the strongside guard so that the guard can pull and lead the quarterback outside toward the perimeter of the defense. This is illustrated in Diagram 7-10.

The strong side guard has three different techniques to execute based on the alignment of the front. If he is uncovered, then he sets for pass protection and pulls to help protect the quarterback on his dash. If both guards are uncovered, then the protection scheme appears as illustrated in Diagram 7-11.

If the strongside guard is covered and the center is uncovered, then the center blocks back so that the strongside guard can set for pass protection and pull. Diagram 7-12 illustrates such a front.

If the center and the strongside guard are both covered, then the strongside guard stays on the man aligned over him and protects as illustrated in Diagram 7-13.

The strongside tackle also has both a covered rule and an uncovered rule. If he is covered, then he takes a deep pass protection set and blocks the man covering him. Diagram 7-14 illustrates this protection scheme.

If the strongside tackle is uncovered, then he protects for the release of the tight end. This is illustrated in Diagram 7-15.

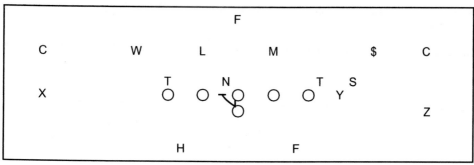

Diagram 7-7: 1 Technique Weak

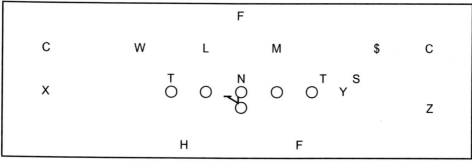

Diagram 7-8: 0 Technique

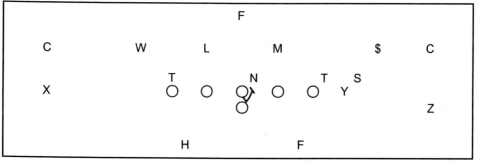

Diagram 7-9: 1 Technique Strong

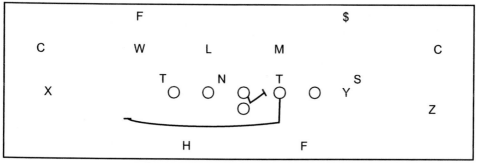

Diagram 7-10: Uncovered Center

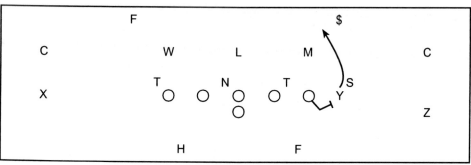

Diagram 7-15: Uncovered Tackle

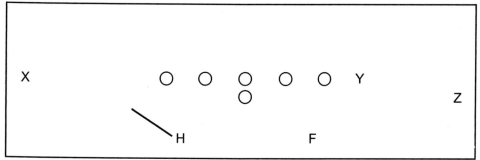

Diagram 7-16: Running Back's Release

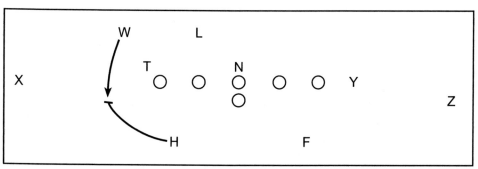

Diagram 7-17: Outside Linebacker

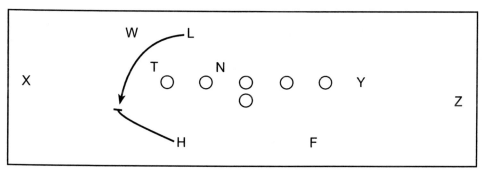

Diagram 7-18: Inside Linebacker

The running backs are an important part of the dash-protection scheme. The running back, on the side of the formation that we are dashing to, must account for any potential threat to the quarterback as he attempts to get outside of the contain element of the defense. The running back must recognize all alignments within the defense and secure the edge of the formation. On the snap of the ball, the running back will gain width and give the appearance that he is releasing on some type of pass route. Diagram 7-16 illustrates the running back's release.

After taking off on his initial release, the running back must maintain control and evaluate the edge of the defensive structure. If any defensive player vacates the weak-side curl or flat zone on a blitz path, then the running back attempts to block him by gaining outside leverage. Diagrams 7-17 and 7-18 illustrate this technique.

If the edge looks secure, then the running back maintains an outside leverage advantage. He should look for a defensive player attempting to break out of coverage to pressure the quarterback to throw the football before he is ready to do so. Diagrams 7-19 and 7-20 illustrate two possibilities.

The offensive coaching staff must prepare the running back to face all of the defensive fronts in which opposing defenses can be expected to line up. The running back must also be able to identify all of the blitzes, coverages, and stunts that the defense likes to use with their front schemes.

The running back on the backside of the formation has a much simpler protection assignment. If the strongside offensive tackle is covered, then the running back will block any wrong-colored jersey that rushes outside of the tackle's initial alignment. This is illustrated in Diagram 7-21.

If the strongside tackle is uncovered, then the running back will utilize scat protection, as described earlier. The running back will identify every potential blitzer who could attack one of the vulnerable unprotected areas of the scheme. The running back scat protects from inside to outside. This technique is illustrated in diagram 7-22.

When using dash-protection schemes, it is imperative that the pass patterns be designed so that the routes are run at a greater depth. The quarterback will not reach his setup point until 2.5 to 4.0 seconds after the snap of the ball. Therefore, the depth of the routes should be adjusted accordingly. Diagrams 7-23 through 7-26 illustrate dash protection against a variety of defensive fronts of fronts.

We can run dash protection to the split-end side of the formation from a variety of formations and looks. Diagrams 7-27 and 7-28 illustrate two possibilities.

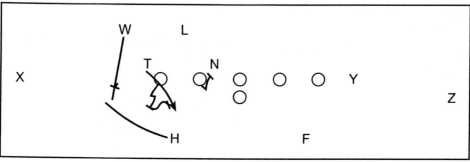

Diagram 7-19: Outside Linebacker

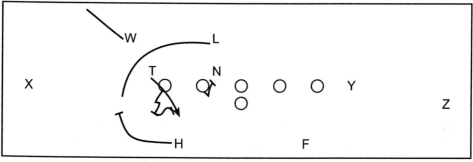

Diagram 7-20: Inside Linebacker

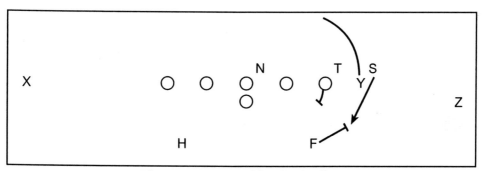

Diagram 7-21: Inside Linebacker

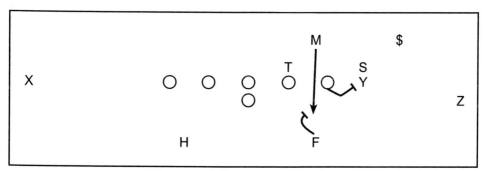

Diagram 7-22: Scat Protection

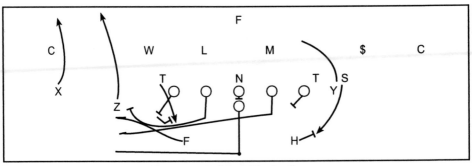

Diagram 7-23: Okie Defense

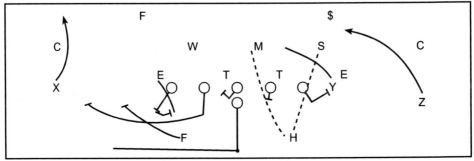

Diagram 7-24: 4-3 Defense

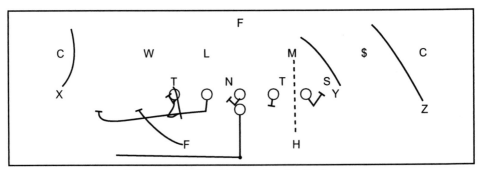

Diagram 7-25: Strong Eagle Defense

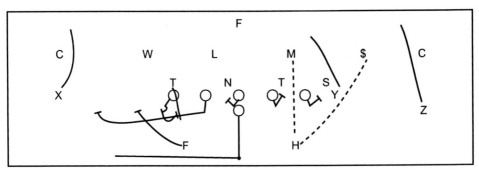

Diagram 7-26: Slide Weak Defense

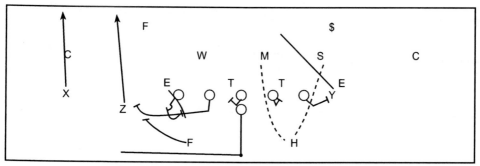

Diagram 7-27: Pro Twins Right Formation

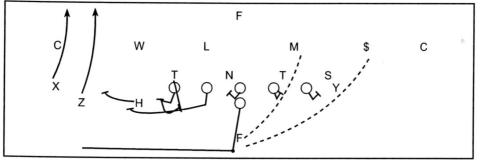

Diagram 7-28: Trips Right Formation

The coaching staff must allocate sufficient time for the quarterback to spend simulating a straight drop-back pass set-up. This action invites the pass rush toward the traditional pocket area before the quarterback releases into his dash path. The quarterback needs to be athletic and fast enough to be able to break contain and get outside. A quarterback who is a threat to run the football in the open field is an asset to teams that want to use dash protection.

CHAPTER 8

PUTTING IT ALL
TOGETHER

If a football team needs to get better at throwing the football because they cannot run it, then that football team is in trouble regardless of the schemes that have been included in this book. It would be a tremendous mistake for any offensive football team to make even minor changes in its current passing attack without giving serious consideration to how these changes will impact their entire offensive package. The most effective offensive football teams are able to exploit defenses by blending the run and the pass into an integrated system of attack. It is NOT a good idea to approach the passing game as an entirely separate part of the offensive attack. Any proposed changes must be discussed within the context of the cadence, formations, motion adjustments, and style of running attack that the offensive unit is currently using.

At the very least, we believe that every offensive football team needs to be able to attack defenses with some form of quick-passing attack and play-action. Regardless of skill level or offensive philosophy, we believe that every offense can develop and implement an effective three-step drop, quick-passing attack without a tremendous amount time and effort. The protection schemes are simple and can be used against a wide variety of defensive fronts. Similarly, it is not a difficult matter to develop some type of play-action scheme that is based on what the offensive team likes to do when they run the football.

The other schemes discussed in this book may or may not be applicable to certain offensive philosophies. It would be foolish to incorporate both dash and sprint-out schemes into your attack, for example, because the goal of both schemes is the same—to get the quarterback outside. While no football team is going to use all of these schemes, we have included them in order to provide coaches with a thorough consideration of each possibility.

It is fairly easy to make an objective evaluation of the effectiveness of an offensive football team's overall style of attack. Put simply, statistics don't lie. Many successful football coaches keep close track of the following:

→ average number of points scored
→ average time of possession
→ average number of turnovers (giveaways)
→ total rushing yards per game

→ total passing yards per game

→ number of quarterback sacks allowed

→ average number of yards per rushing attempt

→ average number of yards per passing attempt

→ pass completion percentage

→ average number of yards gained on first down

→ third-down conversions

While we remain conscious of these statistics, we firmly believe that the most important goal is to win the football game. Because of this, we are more comfortable with poorer offensive statistics (running and passing), when we have confidence in our ability to punt the ball and play solid defense. Sometimes, it is easy for offensive coaches to forget why their teams have been successful. If a program has been built on running the football and playing great defense, then it does not make much sense to begin throwing the football twenty times a game. What we strive to do is to get the most out of our passing game, whenever we do decide to throw the football. We accomplish this by being sound in our protection schemes, and giving our players the opportunity to take advantage of what the defense is doing in order to make a big play.

Personnel have to play a key role in which schemes a football team chooses to run. The dash and sprint-out schemes require a quarterback who possesses some speed and can be a running threat in the open field. Coaches, who have a quarterback with limited arm strength, might want to accommodate him by using a sprint-out scheme. This step provides a shorter throwing distance and allows him to be more effective. The most important factor regarding which scheme to use is the size and the abilities of the offensive linemen. A big, physical line will have more potential success with man schemes, while a smaller group might benefit from zone schemes where they are not asked to overcome physical mismatches.

The number of protection schemes that a coach should include in his playbook is a matter of individual choice. It is for him to decide what is too much and what is not enough. After considering personnel and the strengths and weaknesses of the offensive linemen, the quarterback , and the receivers, the coach needs to decide what his players can accomplish from week to week. Do the opposing defenses play a 4- or 5-man front, blitz their linebackers, or drop them into coverage?

Strong advocates of the running game would probably incorporate a complimentary play-action passing game at the very least. The type may depend on the quarterback. If he is athletic and has good movement skills, the boot and naked schemes will give him an opportunity to use his athletic ability to exploit the run/pass option. If the quarterback has less mobility, then he should set up in the pocket and use a drop-back, play-action passing scheme.

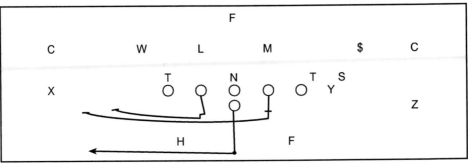

Diagram 7-11: Uncovered Guards

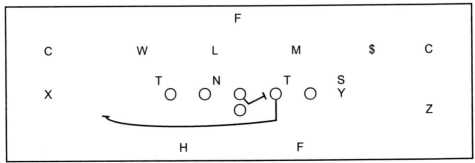

Diagram 7-12: Slide Weak Defense

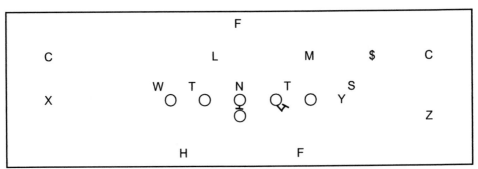

Diagram 7-13: Center and Guard Covered

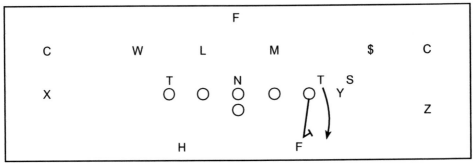

Diagram 7-14: Covered Tackle

If using a more wide-open passing style of offense, a coach should concentrate his protection schemes on the 3- and 5-step variety. How the offense chooses to protect those drops would depend on how complex the passing attack is going to be and on whether three, four, or five receivers will be released.

Coaches that decide to base their offensive attacks on the pass will need to spend a great deal of time on hot reads and blitz adjustments by the quarterback. The passing game needs to be carefully thought out with all parts of the plan able to work effectively together.

Teams that are able to throw the football effectively develop a well thought-out protection scheme and consistent plan of attack, get their players to buy into that plan of attack, and communicate to their players exactly what techniques they need to execute in order for the plan to succeed. It should be kept in mind that football teams do not need to throw the football twenty-five times a game in order to have an effective passing attack. Some of the best offenses in the game throw fewer than ten passes a game. When they do throw the football, however, they are highly effective. In fact, their passing attack is what makes their overall offensive system so hard to defend.

Stan Zweifel is the Assistant Head Football Coach and Offensive Coordinator at the University of Wisconsin-Whitewater. Since joining the Warhawks' staff in 1991, Zweifel has molded the UWW offensive team into one of two leading offenses in the nation. The Warhawks have been nationally ranked in the top 10 in rushing offense, scoring offense, total offense, and passing efficiency for two consecutive years. During his tenure, UWW has had 16 all-conference offensive players, five All-American players and seven players who have gone on to play professional football. Stan has also authored two best-selling coaching books and has produced several well-received instructional videos on offensive football. Stan currently resides in Whitewater, Wisconsin with Diane, his wife of 24 years, and his children—daughters, Saree and Shannon, and sons, Michael and Mark.

Brad Boll is currently an assistant football coach at Beloit Memorial High School in Beloit, Wisconsin. Prior to assuming his present position, Brad coached at Madison Edgewood High School, Vorona High School, Monroe High School, and the University of Wisconsin—Whitewater. At Monroe, his team won a conference championship, while at Madison Edgewood and Beloit, respectively, his teams made the state playoffs. Brad and his wife, Valerie, reside in New Glarus, Wisconsin.

ADDITIONAL FOOTBALL RESOURCES FROM

BOOKS:

■ **101 ZONE OFFENSE PLAYS**
Stan Zweifel
2001 • 128 pp. • ISBN 1-58518-404-7 • $16.95

■ **COACHING FOOTBALL'S ZONE OFFENSE**
Stan Zweifel, Brian Borland, Bob Berezowitz
1998 • 184 pp. • ISBN 1-58518-197-9 • $17.95

■ **101 RECEIVER DRILLS**
Stan Zweifel
1998 • 124 pp. • ISBN 1-58518-205-2 • $16.95

VIDEOS:

■ **FOOTBALL'S ZONE OFFENSE: VOL. 1—INSIDE ZONE RUNNING SCHEMES**
Stan Zweifel
1998 • 90 minutes • ISBN 1-57167-213-3 • $40.00

■ **FOOTBALL'S ZONE OFFENSE: VOL. 2—OUTSIDE ZONE STRETCH SCHEMES**
Stan Zweifel
1998 • 60 minutes • ISBN 1-57167-214-1 • $40.00

■ **FOOTBALL'S ZONE OFFENSE: VOL. 3—PLAY ACTION PASS SCHEMES**
Stan Zweifel
1998 • 60 minutes • ISBN 1-57167-215-X • $40.00

■ **FOOTBALL'S ZONE OFFENSE: VOL. 4—SKILLS AND DRILLS**
Stan Zweifel
1999 • 50 minutes • ISBN 1-57167-359-8 • $40.00

TO PLACE YOUR ORDER:
TOLL FREE (888) 229-5745
MAIL: COACHES CHOICE
 P.O. Box 1828, Monterey, CA 93942
FAX: (831) 393-1102
ONLINE: www.coacheschoiceweb.com